Willem S. Prinsloo

The Theology of the Book of Joel

Willem S. Prinsloo

The Theology
of the Book of Joel

Walter de Gruyter · Berlin · New York

1985

Beiheft zur Zeitschrift für die alttestamentliche Wissenschaft

Herausgegeben von Otto Kaiser

163

Gedruckt mit Unterstützung der Alexander von Humboldt-Stiftung

Library of Congress Cataloging in Publication Data

Prinsloo, Willem S. (Willem Sterrenberg), 1944 –
  The theology of the book of Joel.
  (Beiheft zur Zeitschrift für die alttestamentliche Wissenschaft ;
163)
    Bibliography: p.
    Includes index.
    1. Bible.   O.T.   Joel–Theology.   I. Title.
II. Series.
BS1575.5.P75   1985   224′.706   85-15895
ISBN 0 89925 131 5

CIP-Kurztitelaufnahme der Deutschen Bibliothek

Prinsloo, Willem S.:
The theology of the Book of Joel / Willem S. Prinsloo. –
Berlin ; New York : de Gruyter, 1985.
  (Beiheft zur Zeitschrift für die alttestamentliche Wissenschaft ;
163)
    ISBN 3-11-010301-X
NE: Zeitschrift für die alttestamentliche Wissenschaft / Beiheft

Printed on acid free paper (pH 7, neutral)

©

Preface

I hereby wish to thank prof. dr. Otto Kaiser, the editor of BZAW, and the publishers Walter de Gruyter and Co. for accepting my manuscript for publication in this series.

My sincere thanks to the Alexander von Humboldt-Stiftung not only for the generous stipendium which enabled me to carry out a research project at the University of Tübingen, but also for a financial assistance towards the printing of this book.

My heartfelt thanks to prof. dr. H. Gese and prof. dr. S. Mittmann and other members of the Evangelisch-Theologische Fakultät, Tübingen. I not only profited by their seminars, the well equipped library and academic discussions, but we were also inundated by them with kindness and friendship during our stay in Tübingen.

Pretoria   Willem S. Prinsloo

Contents

Abbreviations

I. Introduction

Old Testament theology today is passing through a phase of enormous growth as well as something of a crisis. The crisis is due to a total lack of consensus, even about the so-called "basic issues" of this science.[1]

The growth has been stimulated by several new Old Testament theologies published in recent years and a lively discussion on problem areas in this field.[2]

This study in no way professes to offer a solution to these problems. At most it is a contribution to the current debate and an attempt at offering a fresh slant on the questions.

To speak of *a* theology of the Old Testament simply will not do: one has to allow for several such theologies.[3] The Old Testament is a many-faceted book with a long and intricate history and every attempt to pin its theology down to a single structure has been abortive. Virtually all such efforts have been based on broad themes or trends, with the result that parts of the Old Testament have been either overemphasized or neglected — and some parts completely overlooked.[4] All attemps at categorizing the contents of the Old Testament according to some dogmatic system must likewise be rejected, as must endeavours at focusing those contents around a so-called *Mitte*. Using such a *Mitte* — whether explicitly or implicitly — again results in underaccentuation of certain parts, or in forcing them into a contrived framework. In addition the *Mitte* usually constitutes a highly subjective research premise and the researcher's assumptions — both methodological and confessional — play a far greater part than is commonly conceded.

---

[1] Cf. G. F. Hasel, Old Testament Theology, Basic issues in the current debate, ³1982.

[2] Cf. Hasel, op. cit.; H. G. Reventlow, Hauptprobleme der alttestamentlichen Theologie im 20. Jahrhundert, 1982; H. Seebaß, Biblische Theologie, Beihefte zu EvTh 27 (1/82), for a complete list and a discussion of the latest publications.

[3] Cf. W. S. Prinsloo, The Theology of Jeremiah 27:1−11, OTWSA 24 (1981), 67.

[4] Cf. e.g. R. E. Clements, Old Testament Theology, A fresh approach, 1978 who does not pay any attention to wisdom literature.

A more acceptable way would be to try and determine the theology of individual Old Testament documents or "blocks of writings".[5] Theoretically this should enable one to arrive at a synthesis of Old Testament theology, but whether this is actually feasible is another matter. The fact remains that in writing such a theology one must start, not with the superstructure, but with the basics — that is the individual books or "blocks of writings". When we speak of theologies "we naturally do not mean a number of disparate theologies which have nothing to do with one another. We prefer to see such theologies as a multifaceted diamond with countless dimensions"[6]. The fundamental unity of the various Old Testament Theologies arises from the fact that they all form part of the same canon and tell of the same God, Yahweh.[7]

In this study we shall be concentrating on the theology of the book of Joel. By "theology" we mean *what the book Joel tells us about Yahweh*. Hence a theology of the book of Joel is not intended to present a systematized, static or isolated image of Yahweh, but a synthesis of the "picture of Yahweh" reflected in this book. We reiterate: this theology does not set out to construe a one-sided image of Yahweh but will try to adhere to the contents of the book.

Another point to be noted is that this is a theology of the *book of Joel* — not of the prophet Joel, nor of the "apocalyptic" or any other redactor. Our point of departure is the final form of the text of this book. The text as we have it today is the object of study. Historical criticism must face the charge that, on the strength of its romantic supposition that the earliest source is the most authentic or the best, it has often failed to take proper account of the final text. In its attempt at reconstructing the so-called "original" text it makes so much of the origin and growth of the final version that the latter is largely neglected.

The honest exegete embarking on a study of the book of Joel faces a host of problems. The *first* and probably the greatest of these concerns the *redaction history, composition* and *structure* of the book. This problem was first raised in 1872 by the French scholar M. Vernes,[8] who believed that the

---

[5] Hasel, op. cit., 93; cf. also W. S. Prinsloo, The Theology of the book of Ruth, VT 30 (1980), 330—341.

[6] W. S. Prinsloo, OTWSA 24 (1981), 67.

[7] Cf. H. G. Reventlow, Grundfragen der alttestamentlichen Theologie, TZ 17 (1961), 96 who writes: "Die wirkliche Mitte ist im Alten Testament keine andere als im Neuen: es ist der sich selbst offenbarende Gott."

[8] Le peuple d'Israël et ses espérances, cf. especially 46—54.

first half (chapters 1 and 2) tells of a *Yom Yahweh* that has come and gone, whereas the second half (chapters 3 and 4) speaks of a *Yom* still to come. Accordingly Vernes argues that the book must have been written by two separate authors. In 1896 J. W. Rothstein,[9] again emphasizing the differences between Joel 1–2 and 3–4, dated the first part before the exile and gave the second a postexilic dating.

The most influential theory, however, was that of B. Duhm,[10] whose approach became the classical literary-critical model for the interpretation of the book of Joel. Although he modified this thesis over the years, his basic standpoint remained unchanged: the prophet Joel was personally responsible for chapters 1 and 2 only, the section written in verse and telling of a plague of locusts. Chapters 3 and 4 are apocalyptic additions by a synagogal preacher from Maccabean times. Duhm avers that this latter section was written in prose form. But according to him even chapters 1 and 2 cannot be attributed wholly to Joel. The apocalyptic redactor introduced various interpretations into these chapters, namely 1 15; 2 1b–2a and 2 11b. In this way, Duhm believes, one can arrive at the authentic *Urschrift* of the book of Joel.

Duhm's hypothesis of the development of Joel was tremendously influential among researchers of this book, many of whom subscribed to it. R. E. Wolfe[11] took historical criticism to the point of the absurd with his "Anti-neighbour editor" (4 4–11 and 13), "Day of Yahweh editor" (1 15; 2 1d–2b; 2 10–11; 3 1–5; 4 1–3; 4 14–17), "Eschatologists" (4 18–19 and 21a) and "Psalm editor" (4 20 and 21b). These various "editors" were all said to have made certain additions. *H. Birkeland*[12] too accepted Duhm's ideas: Joel 1 and 2 should be seen as a description of a past event and Joel 3 and 4 as a secondary addition. Because of the addition of 3 and 4 and redactional changes to 1 and 2 the latter were also transformed into prophecies for the future.

Duhm's views profoundly influenced the commentaries on Joel that were published subsequently: J. A. Bewer,[13] E. Sellin[14] and T. H. Robin-

[9] Cf. S. R. Driver, Einleitung in die Literatur des AT, 333ff. – edit. by J. W. Rothstein.
[10] Cf. Theologie der Propheten, 1875, 275–277; Anmerkungen zu den Zwölf Propheten, ZAW 31 (1911), 184–187.
[11] The editing of the book of the Twelve, ZAW 53 (1935), 90–129.
[12] Zum hebräischen Traditionswesen. Die Komposition der prophetischen Bücher des Alten Testaments, 1938, 64–66.
[13] The book of Joel, ICC, 1911.
[14] Joel, das Zwölfprophetenbuch, 1929.

son[15] are all to some extent disciples of Duhm's. One should always bear this background in mind when using or evaluating a commentary.

To complicate matters further the views of Duhm and his followers provoked a strong reaction. This other school of Joel scholars placed more emphasis on the *unity* of the book. *L. Dennefeld*[16] discerned a single underlying idea indicative of a single author. *J. H. Kritzinger*[17] likewise stressed the unity of the book. *A. S. Kapelrud*[18] although adhering to the oral transmission of Joel, nonetheless postulated a single liturgical function for the entire book. He associated it with the so-called enthronement feast of Yahweh. Kapelrud contrary to the classical historical-critical model, endorsed the unity of the book. In similar fashion *Th. Chary*[19] built on the theory of his French compatriot Dennefeld and stressed the unity of Joel.

Most of the commentaries to have appeared over the past few decades also proceed from the unity of the book of Joel. The more important ones were those by *D. Deden*,[20] *J. A. Thompson*,[21] *A. Weiser*,[22] *C. A. Keller*,[23] *W. Rudolph*[24] and, most recently, *L. C. Allen*.[25] Among recent commentaries that by H. W. Wolff[26] was, however, the most significant. Wolff demonstrated the literary symmetry of the book as a whole, which in his view strongly suggests a single author. *B. S. Childs*,[27] although considering Joel to be a literary unity, does not attribute this fact to a single author but rather to a final redactor who consciously forged the book into a redactional entity.

These excerpts from the research history of the book of Joel indicate quite clearly that its unity and origin pose a real problem. Fortunately of late the pendulum appears to have swung back in the direction of a unified

---

[15] Die Zwölf kleinen Propheten, HAT 14, ³1964.

[16] Les problèmes du livre de Joel, RSR 4 (1924), 555–575.

[17] Die profesie van Joël, 1935.

[18] Joel studies, 1948; cf. also G. S. Ogden, Joel 4 and prophetic responses to national laments, JSOT 26 (1983), 98 who in a recent article also advocates the unity of Joel: "One implication of the view that Joel is a unity is that a definable relationship exists between the later chapters and what precedes in terms of the ritual of lamentation".

[19] Les Prophetes et le Culte, à partir de l'exil, 1955, 190–216.

[20] De kleine profeten, BOT, 1953.

[21] The Interpreter's Bible, 6, 1956.

[22] Das Buch der Zwölf Kleinen Propheten, ATD 24/1, 1956.

[23] Joel, Commentaire de l'ancien Testament XI/a, 1965.

[24] Joel – Amos – Obadja – Jona, KAT XIII/2, 1971.

[25] The books of Joel, Obadiah, Jonah and Micah, NICOT, 1976.

[26] Dodekapropheton (Joel und Amos), BKAT IV/2, 1975.

[27] Introduction to the Old Testament as Scripture, 1979, ad loc.

book. An exception to this diagnosis is that of *Otto Plöger*,[28] who regards the transmission and redaction history of the book of Joel[29] thus: chapters 1 and 2 contain a written record of the oral message of the prophet Joel, the plague of locusts being augmented and reinterpreted by the tradition of the *Yom Yahweh* to give it eschatological overtones. The metaphorical assertions concerning the Yom Yahweh in chapters 1 and 2 are furthermore eschatologically interpreted by the addition of chapter 4. In chapter 4 the concern is no longer with cultic affairs (as in chapters 1 and 2), but with an eschatological interpretation of Yahweh's intervention in history. Subsequently chapter 3 was inserted to set a sort of limitation, in that the promises of chapter 4 were confined to Israel only.

As we have shown, Plöger's viewpoint is somewhat out of step with the overall trend in current research.

A *second problem*, and one possibly attended by even greater confusion, is that of the *dating of Joel*. A further distinction could be made between the dating of the *prophet's lifetime* and that of the writing of the *book*. The remarkable thing is that exegetes proceed from exactly the same data, yet manage to arrive at widely divergent findings. One likely reason is that the preconceptions – particularly as regards method – of these scholars play a far greater role than they are prepared to admit. Thus in most cases the questions addressed to the text predetermine the answers. Often such a "prefabricated" dating decides the exegesis of the book, determining the scholar's whole approach to the text and resulting in a completely circular argument. This is to be avoided. If after searching scrutiny the text itself offers no definite pointers as regards dating, the researcher should be honest enough to admit defeat.

An overview of the various attempts at dating the book reveals the following astonishing picture: *K. A. Credner*,[30] who dated Joel before the exile – during the reign of king Joash of Judah in the 9th century B. C. – led the field for quite a long time. Such a dating would accord well with Joash's youth when the high priest Jehoiada acted as regent (II Reg 11–12), for the book of Joel makes no mention of any king. Another argument favouring a pre-exilic dating is the positioning of Joel between Amos and Hosea in the collection of so-called Minor Prophets. This would indicate an early origin. Such scholars as *G. C. Aalders*[31] and *E. J. Young*[32] supported Credner's

---

[28] Theocratie und Eschatologie, 1959.
[29] Op. cit., 117–128.
[30] Der Prophet Joel, 1831, 40ff.
[31] Oud Testamentische Kanoniek, 1952, 252–254.
[32] An introduction to the Old Testament, 1949, 271ff.

pre-exilic dating. Interestingly Miloš Bič[33] advances very different reasons
for the same dating, namely the reign of King Joash of Judah (836—797
B.C.). Bič maintains that in Joel we have an *"uralten Text"* dating back to
the struggle against Baalism and reflecting the Judaen phase of this confron-
tation.

Some scholars espouse a late pre-exilic dating. *A. S. Kapelrud*[34] believes that Joel must have lived in the reign of King Zedekiah and that the
book originated round 600 B.C. For the first three centuries, however, it
was transmitted orally and was recorded only in the 3rd century B.C. *C. A.
Keller*[35] dates Joel's ministry to 630—600 B.C. and believes that 4 19 refers
to Egyptian aggression in the 7th century B.C. *Klaus Koch*[36] also assigns a
dating towards the end of the 7th century, during the Assyrian overlordship
shortly before Assyria fell in 612 B.C. *W. Rudolph*[37] advances various arguments for dating Joel's ministry to the period 597—587 B.C.

The majority of exegetes, however, settle for an *exilic or postexilic dating of* Joel. The main arguments are as follows:[38] no major enemies of Judah
are mentioned, hence the book should be dated at the earliest after the fall of
Babylon in 539 B.C.; the historical references in 4 2 ff. are seen as indicating
the fall of Jerusalem in 587 B.C.; the book of Joel's positive evaluation of
the cultus is seen as contrasting with the critical attitude of pre-exilic
prophets; the absence of a king and the prominence of the priesthood are
also cited as proof of a postexilic dating; the fact that the entire population
could be summoned to the temple (see 2 1) leads some scholars to believe
that this was the tiny postexilic community; the terminology referring to
offerings (see 1 9 and 13; 2 14) is considered typically postexilic; the reference to a wall in 2 7 is said to indicate that Joel must have originated after
Nehemiah had reconstructed the walls of Jerusalem, hence after 445 B.C.;
the reference to the Greeks in 4 6f. indicates a time after the start of the
Persian rule. Linguistic data are also cited in favour of a postexilic dating.
As far back as the last century *H. Holzinger*[39] observed that the language of
Joel would suggest that it is one of the last of the Old Testament books. The

---

[33] Das Buch Joel, 1969, 106—108.
[34] Op. cit., 191—192.
[35] Op. cit., 103—104.
[36] K. Koch, Die Propheten I, Assyrische Zeit, 1978, 171.
[37] Cf. KAT XIII/2, 1971, 24—29 and Wann wirkte Joel?, BZAW 105 (1967), 193—198. Cf.
    also W. Beyerlin, "Wir sind wie Träumende". Studien zum 126. Psalm (Stuttgarter Bibel-
    studien 89), 1978, 57, who supports the view of Rudolph.
[38] Cf. Allen, op. cit., 20—21.
[39] ZAW 9 (1889), 92, 129.

fact that Joel quotes from other prophetic books[40] is also seen as evidence of its postexilic origin.

If one studies the arguments for a postexilic dating more closely, the picture that emerges is somewhat confused. The facts indicate not one specific time during the exile, but a protracted period. This is particularly marked when one examines some individual datings: *W. F. Albright*[41] dates the book between 522 and 517 B.C. *J. M. Myers*[42] takes Albright's arguments further, maintaining that the facts of the book of Joel suggest the period of Haggai and Zechariah and reflect the Palestinian situation round 520 B.C. *Bo Reicke*[43] cites particularly 4 8f. in evidence of a dating round 520 B.C. After lengthy argument *G. W. Ahlström*[44] arrives at the following conclusion: "Having seen that the cult of the second temple cannot have been free from the accusation of being syncretistic and idolatrous, it is therefore possible to maintain that the period between 515 and 445 B.C. is the period which can suit the requirements of the evidence for the date of Joel." *I. H. Eybers*[45] concludes that Joel should be dated after the reconstruction of the temple in 516 B.C., but before 460 B.C. According to *H. W. Wolff*[46] all the evidence points to the cultic community of the days of Ezra and Nehemiah, hence between 445 and 343 B.C.

A. Weiser[47] maintains that 1 14; 2 7f. and 3 5 indicate that Jerusalem's walls must already have been rebuilt, hence he dates the book after Nehemiah, round 400 B.C. *J. Morgenstern*[48] argues that 4 2−8 and 4 19−20 refer, not to the Babylonian exile of 587 B.C., but to a time when a coalition of nations (including Tyre and Sidon) traded in individual Jewish slaves. This period is said to have been between 490 and 465 B.C., but the events were not recorded until 411 B.C. *H. Birkeland*[49] also believes that the book of Joel was not recorded until relatively late − the 4th or 5th centuries B.C., in fact. *J. A. Bewer*[50] makes an interesting attempt to assign separate datings

---

[40] Cf. e.g. Isa 13 6 with 1 15; Ez 30 2ff. with 1 15; Zeph 1 14ff. with 2 1ff.; Mal 3 2 with 2 11; Ob 17 with 4 17.

[41] JBL 61 (1942), 120ff.

[42] Some considerations bearing on the date of Joel, ZAW 74 (1962), 177−195.

[43] Joel und seine Zeit, Wort − Gebot − Glaube, Walter Eichrodt zum 80. Geburtstag, 1970, 133−144.

[44] Joel and the temple cult of Jerusalem, SVT 21 (1971), 129.

[45] Dating Joel's prophecies, Theologia Evangelica Vol. V−VII (1972−74), 219.

[46] BKAT XIV/2, 3−4.

[47] Op. cit., 106.

[48] The testimony of Joel 4, 2b−8, 19−20, HUCA XXVII (1956), 150−153.

[49] Op. cit., 66.

[50] Op. cit., 56−62.

for the prophet Joel, the so-called eschatological redactor and the author of
4 4–8. He sums up:[51] "The book of Joel was completed by the middle of
the 4th century B.C. If we place Joel himself at about 400 B.C. and the
editor a few decades later we shall probably not be far off the mark."
Whether one concurs with Bewer's datings or not, the fact remains that he
is one of the very few scholars who does not simply assign a blanket dating,
but tries to distinguish between the life of the prophet and that of the redaction of the book. *F. R. Stephenson*[52] uses so-called astronomical data (3 4)
to arrive at a dating round 350 B.C. – in fact, he claims that this is the
dating accepted by most Joel scholars![53] In view of the above research history one wonders if this claim is not perhaps a trifle presumptuous. At all
events, it is quite inadmissible to treat the data in Joel as if they derive from
some astronomy textbook and then use them to "solve" the problem of
dating the book. *Marco Treves*[54] believes that Joel 4 19 may be used to date
the book to the reign of Ptolemy, son of Lagus, who ruled Egypt from 323
to 285 B.C.[55] ". . . when the northern tribes had disappeared, the Jews were
scattered among the nations, the temple was functioning, Mount Zion was
the only holy mountain, the wall was standing, the priests ruled Jerusalem,
the Jews had no armies. Egypt oppressed Judea, and the Greeks bought
Jewish slaves."

B. Duhm[56] feels that Joel may be dated to the 4th, 3rd or even the 2nd
century. The larger part of the book (2 18–4 21), plus some minor additions (1 13–15; 2 1–3 and 11), were not written until the 2nd century. Of
course Duhm's dating correlates closely with his conception of the redaction history of the book.

This cursory survey of attempts at dating Joel reveals that the book has
been dated variously from the 9th to the 2nd century B.C. – a period of
seven centuries. Yet each scholar seems to be totally confident of his facts
and able to cite evidence to prove them. It would also seem that the researchers made little distinction between the prophet's lifetime and the period of origin of the book: the two datings are lumped together and presented
in an undifferentiated way. Yet it stands to reason that the historical and the
literary *Sitz im Leben* of the book need not necessarily coincide.

---

[51] Op. cit., 61–62.
[52] The date of the book of Joel, VT 19 (1969), 224–229.
[53] Op. cit., 229.
[54] The date of Joel, VT 7 (1957), 149–156.
[55] Op. cit., 153.
[56] B. Duhm, Israels Propheten, ²1922, 398.

Despite the importance of a definite dating for the interpretation of any book – including Joel – it seems pointless to add yet another (subjective!) attempt to the host of proposed datings. It seems more fitting simply to admit that the data in the book of Joel do not permit such a dating.[57] Thereupon one should use the substance of the book to the best possible effect to discover its actual purpose and message. That, after all, is the main aim of exegesis.

Could one of our greatest problems not perhaps be that we use *extra-textual* evidence to decide issues such as dating, whereas the content of the text itself is largely ignored? This certainly applies to the research history of the book of Joel. *B. S. Childs*[58] makes a significant point when he says about Joel: "The crucial issue turns on how one reads the book in its present form."

Of course, if one takes the final text as one's point of departure one may, at the other extreme, get trapped in a sort of ahistorical, impressionistic method, which would be equally one-sided.

Our aim here is to *combine theology with exegesis as much as we can. Exegesis must guide us to a meaningful synthesis of what the text of Joel has to say about Yahweh.* We reiterate, we are not speaking of theology in the sense of a systematic doctrine of God. And even though we shall naturally have to scrutinize the whole book of Joel minutely, this study is not a commentary on – or a verse-by-verse interpretation of – Joel. The intention is to focus on its theology. Nor does theology mean an actualization of the message of the book in the sense of its significance for people today. In speaking of a theology of Joel we are using this word in its literal sense.

Although we shall not be following a rigid order of exegetical steps, the basic sequence will be synchronic – diachronic.[59] The book will be discussed pericope by pericope. Syntactic analysis will provide a verifiable framework for the overall exegetic process. Hence structure serves not as structuralists would have it, but simply as a means to an end. The diachronic aspects are no less important. Here historical criticism can be applied to good effect so as to analyse the historical process underlying Joel inasmuch as the text permits this.

On the one hand all the diachronic aspects must be borne in mind. After all, the book has an intricate transmission and redaction history in

---

[57] P. A. Verhoef, Die Dag van die Here, Exegetica 2/3, 1956, 49.
[58] Op. cit., 389.
[59] For a brief methodological account see W. S. Prinsloo, Isaiah 14 12–15, Humiliation, Hubris, Humiliation, ZAW 93 (1981), 432 ff.

which various traditions and theological trends must have featured. Obviously these factors will have to be taken into account if we are to understand the theology of Joel.

On the other hand, if a text should offer no clear clues to diachronic problems, the researcher must acknowledge this frankly. He must be wary of introducing extratextual evidence, but should make maximum use of the text — noting both synchronic and diachronic aspects — so as to arrive at a meaningful approval of the theology of the book of Joel.

There is no short cut to the theology of a book: it must be built block by block from the ground up!

II. 1 1

(1) deⱱăr-jhwh ʾªšær hajah ʾæl-jôʾel bæn-petûʾel

This stich provides the heading for the entire book. It is demarcated from the next stich because the latter (1 2) starts with a *conventional introductory formula* (šimeᶜû), marking a new pericope.

Hence 1 1 is treated as a separate unit. This stich could fairly be called a *standard formula*.[1] Its basic form deⱱăr-jhwh ʾªšær hajah ʾæl, corresponds with Hos 1 1; Mi 1 1 and Zeph 1 1 (cf. also Jer 1 2; Ez 1 3; Jon 1 1; Sach 1 1; I Sam 15 10; II Sam 24 11), but Joel 1 1 differs from the other three prophetic books in that the introductory formula is not followed by a historical framework. To infer from this omission[2] "... that Joel's ministry was so comparatively recent as to be well known to the readers and so not requiring specification" would be reading too much into the text. Hence one cannot deduce anything about the prophet's historical *Sitz im Leben* from this abrupt introduction. Attempts at attaching symbolic significance to the name Joel − on the basis of its *"Grundbedeutung"* − must likewise be rejected.

What the heading tells us quite plainly − and for our purpose this is significant − is that what follows is qualified as the word of Yahweh. The prophet, acting as intermediary, assumes a secondary place.

The first stich, the heading for the book as a whole, indicates that everything below it is the authoritative word of Yahweh.

---

[1] Both H. W. Wolff, Dodekapropheton I, Hosea (BKAT XIV/1), 196, 2 and A. S. van der Woude, Micha (POT), 1976, 13 point out that this formula occurs in Deuteronomic circles.
[2] L. C. Allen, (NICOT), 45.

III. 1 2—14

There is no agreement on the *demarcation* of this pericope. Many interpreters would like to have a new pericope start at 1 13[1] but there are plausible arguments for accepting 1 2—14 as a demarcated pericope.

The beginning of the pericope is undisputed: 1 2a starts with a conventional introductory formula (šimᵉᶜû), setting it apart from the heading of the book in 1 1.

The passage 1 2—14 is *integral* in the sense that 1 2 and 1 14 show a striking resemblance. The many *lexeme recurrences* and word-plays (see detailed discussion) also suggest a unified passage. *Formally* too there are correspondences, notably the imperatives (1 5a; 1 8; 1 11a; 1 13a; 1 13b; 1 14a; 1 14b); the concomitant vocatives (1 5a; 1 11a; 1 13a); and the high frequency of kî. These attributes also mark the pericope as a summons to national lamentation (see detailed discussion below).

Although 1 15ff. has links with the preceding verses, it introduces a completely new *theme*, namely the Yom Yahweh. Besides, the high-frequency imperatives of the first pericope are absent from 1 15a, the metre of which also differs markedly from that of the preceding verses.

---

[1] Cf. D. W. Nowack, Die kleinen Propheten (HAT III/4), ³1922, 92; D. R. Jones, Isaiah 56—66 and Joel (Torch Bible Commentaries), 1964, 133 and 141ff. A. S. Kapelrud, Joel Studies, 1948, 4, maintains that "... both sections, vv. 2—12 and 13—20 are integrant and must be considered as a larger whole", but he still distinguishes between vv. 12 and 13. Kapelrud's demarcation is governed by subjective exaggeration of the cultic character of Joel. He sees 1 13—20 as a "liturgic unity" (cf. 5). Cf. also Miloš Bič, Das Buch Joel, 1960, 34. L. C. Allen, op. cit., 53, although he also wants a new pericope to start at 1 13, concedes that this pericope contains an intensification of the preceding "service of lamentation". If so, why start a new pericope at 1 13. Rudolph, KAT XIII/2, 46 also starts a new pericope at 1 13 and writes: "Der Aufbau ist formal zunächst derselbe wie in den drei vorhergehenden Unterabschnitten, aber inhaltlich führt der Abschnitt weiter." Of course Rudolph is quite right in claiming that there are formal resemblances between 1 13ff. and the preceding section, but these in fact militate against starting a new pericope at 1 13. The fact that 1 13 "inhaltlich weiter führt" is no criterion for starting a new pericope at this point. Each of the preceding strophes manifest a progression on the content of the strophes immediately before them.

Hence both form and content afford grounds for demarcating 1 2–14 as a separate pericope comprising several strophes, namely 2a–4b; 5a–7b; 8–10b; 11a–12c and 13a–14c. A striking feature is that each strophe starts with an imperative. As for the interrelationship of the various strophes, it may be noted that 1 2a–4b acts as an introduction to 1 5a–14c. The former is a general invocation, whereas 1 5a–14c is more specific, addressing particular strata of the population.

There are no grounds for starting a new pericope at 1 13a. Apart from the fact that 1 13ff. correlates with the preceding verses as regards form, content and *Gattung*, 1 13–14 appears to correspond chiastically with 1 8–10 and 1 11–12 (cf. discussion, p. 23 below). Let us now consider the structure of the various strophes.

(1) 1 2a–4b

```
┌  2a   šimᵉʿû-zoʾt hăzzᵉqenîm wᵉhăʾᵃzînû kol jôšᵉbê haʾaræṣ
│ ┌─2b   hæhajᵉtā zoʾt bîmêkæm wᵉ ʿim bîmê ʾᵃbotêkæm
├─┤─3a   ʿalæhā libnêkæm săpperû ûbᵉnêkæm libnêhæm────────┐
│ └─3b   ûbᵉnêhæm lᵉdôr ʾăher ─────────────────────────────┘
└─┌─4a   jætær hăggazam ʾakăl haʾărbæh wᵉjætær haʾărbæh ʾakăl hăjjalæq
  └─4b   wᵉjætær hăjjælæq ʾakăl hæhasîl
```

The *structure* of the first strophe (2a–4b) is as follows: 2a–3b are closely linked by the incidence of the imperatives, šimᵉʿû, hăʾᵃzînû in 2a and săpperû in 3a. *3a and 3b* are interlinked since they combine to form a single colon.[2] The *waw* copulative at 3b is also striking. There is a further close connection between 2b and 3a: At ʿalæhā in 3a we have a pronominal suffix repetition of zoʾt in 2b, the second person plural suffixes (bîmêkæm, ʾᵃbotêkæm) establish a further connection between 2b and 3a. This goes hand and hand with the conspicuous rhyme of 2b and 3a: ʾᵃbotêkæm, libnêhæm. 2b/3a, 3b link up with the preceding 2a: at 2b we find a repetition and a closer specification of zoʾt in 2a.

Logically *4a and 4b* are interlinked: jætær is repeated thrice and on each occasion is followed by ʾakăl. In addition 4a and 4b are connected by a

---

[2] Here "colon" is used in the sense of a syntactic unit comprising an independent verbal and nominal element. Cf. J. P. Louw, Semantiek van Nuwe Testamentiese Grieks, 1976, especially 78ff.

waw copulative. Thematically too, the two stichs treat of the same topic, to wit the locusts. Lines 4a/4b link up with the preceding in that they specify in more detail the event hitherto referred to as zo't (2a, 2b).[3]

The author uses various stylistic devices to stress the momentousness of his announcement and the magnitude of the catastrophe. The three imperatives, šimᵉᶜû, hăᵃzînû, săpperû, highlight the portentousness of the tidings. The rhetorical question at 3a and the emphatic position of ᶜalæhā accentuate the extraordinary and unique character of the event.[4] In both 3a/b and 4a/b he uses anadiplosis[5] to underscore the succession of generations and swarms of locusts. This reiterative, cumulative style[6] mounts steadily to a climax in 4a/4b, where the triple use of the perfect (ᵓakăl) the "Faktizität des Geschehens betont".[7] The nature and significance of the locusts in 4a/4b have been much — perhaps too much — discussed[8] and diverse explanations have been given. The text itself affords no material for any inferences about the nature of the locusts. We accept the conclusion of Miloš Bič:[9] "Der Prophet dachte sicher nicht an verschiedene Entwicklungsstufen der Heuschrecken, sondern er wollte die Unüberwindlichkeit dieses Feindes betonen, dem nichts entgehen wird, vor dem niemand flüchten kann."

The *metre* of the book of Joel could, by and large, be described as diversified. Sellin[10] observes: "Man wird nur sagen können, daß der Rhythmus ... regelloser ist als der meisten früheren Propheten." This comment naturally applies to chapter 1 as well.[11] Yet with regard to 1 4 one could argue that the gravity of the catastrophe is further accentuated by the longer metre.

---

[3] J. A. Bewer, Joel, (ICC), 1974, 74; C. A. Keller, Joël, Abdias, Jonas, (Commentaire de l'Ancien Testament XI/a), 1965, 109.

[4] Bewer, op. cit., 76.

[5] J. A. Thompson, The book of Joel (IB 6), 1956, 737; J. A. Thompson, The use of repetition in the prophecy of Joel (*in* On language, culture and religion: In honor of E. A. Nida), 1974, 106.

[6] Allen, op. cit., 49.

[7] Wolff, BKAT XIV/2, 32.

[8] Cf. Wolff, BKAT XIV/2, 30—32 for an exposition; also Allen, op. cit., 49—50, footnotes 19 and 20; Rudolph, KAT XIII/2, 40—41.

[9] Bič, op. cit., 16—17.

[10] E. Sellin, Das Zwölfprophetenbuch, ³1929, 150.

[11] The following proposals have been made concerning the metre of 1 2—4 by Allen, op. cit., 46; Bewer, op. cit., 74; and T. H. Robinson, Die Zwölf Kleinen Propheten (HAT 14), ³1964, 59 respectively:

The *Gattung* of the first strophe, 1 2—4, may be defined as a conventional *Lehreröffnungsruf*[12] which, due to the concatenation of elements, displays a certain likeness to wisdom literature.[13] The communication of facts to coming generations (3a/b) is reminiscent of the paranetic passages in Deuteronomy which concern the same principle (see Dtn 4 9; 6 6ff.; 32 7ff.). This *Lehreröffnungsruf* helps to emphasize the importance of the announcement that follows.

This strophe does not reflect any *traditions* in the proper sense. Categoric pronouncements about the *redaction history* of the book of Joel — which includes 1 2—4 — are a risky undertaking.[14] The statement that 1 2—4 constitutes a literary introduction to the original orally transmitted 1 5—2 27 is unsubstantiated and unacceptable.

This introductory strophe stresses the magnitude, severity and unique character of the catastrophe — the plague of locusts — and the portentousness of the message is *inter alia* brought home by the *Lehreröffnungsruf*. It is a general invocation heard by all, but also to be passed on to future generations.

	Allen	Bewer	Robinson
2a	3+3	3+3	3+3
2b	3+3	3+2	3+3
3a	3+2	3+2	3+3
3b	3	3	—
4a	4+4 ⎫	3+3 ⎫	2+2, 2+2
4b	+4 ⎭	+3 ⎭	2+2

[12] Wolff, BKAT XIV/2, 8; A. Deissler, Zwölf Propheten, Hosea. Joël. Amos, (NEB 4), 1981, 69. Cf. e. g. Hos 5 1; Dtn 32 1; Ps 78 1; Isa 1 10; H. G. Reventlow, Prophetisches Ich bei Jeremia, 1962, 116 and W. Baumgartner, Joel 1 und 2, BZAW 34, 10 calls it "Aufforderung zum Horen".

[13] Cf. Wolff, op. cit., 29ff.; H.-P. Müller, Prophetie und Apokalyptik bei Joel, Theologia Viatorum 10 (1965/66), 233.

[14] Cf. W. S. Prinsloo, Die boek Joël: Verleentheid of geleentheid?, NGTT XXIV (1983), 255—258.

(2) 1 5—7

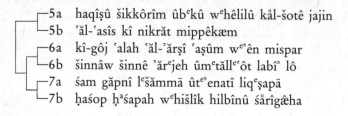

We have shown that 1 5a—7b form a strophe or section within the pericope 1 2—14. It distinguishes itself from the preceding strophe in that the invocation is no longer universal but is specified and directed to a particular section of the community.

The only *text-critical* problem occurs at 7b: ḥaśop ḫᵃśapah wᵉhišlîk. The absence of any suffix to the verb hišlîk strikes one as peculiar, so that it would be grammatically more correct to read the infinitive absolute haślek.[15]

The *structure* of 5a—7b is as follows: The most remarkable feature of 5a is the three consecutive imperatives, which clearly serve an emphatic function. By contrast with 2—4 where the summons is directed to the people generally, these imperatives are addressed to a specific group, kål-šotê jajin, the winebibbers or drunkards. C. A. Keller is probably correct in claiming that "les impératifs marquent un mouvement, une gradation".[16] Verse 5b links up with 5a, ᶜᵃl indicating what is to be bewailed, with the substantiating kî in the latter half of the stich stating the actual reason for the injunctions or imperatives: the winebibbers have been deprived of their wine.

At 6a one finds another motivative kî giving the reason why there is no wine harvest. Thus 6a links up with the combination 5a/5b. But there are weightier reasons why 6a—7b constitute an even closer unity, for they consistently share the same subject, gôj. In addition the verbs of all three these stichs are in the perfect tense: ᶜalah — 6a; šam — 7a; ḥaśop — 7b, stressing the finality of the action of the gôj. The first person singular suffixes in this section are particularly striking: ʾărṣî — 6a; găpnî, tᵉᵒenatî — 7a. In the same

---

[15] Cf. BHS ad loc.; BHK³ ad loc.; T. H. Robinson, op. cit., 58; Sellin, op. cit., 151. Cf. also Rudolph's comments in KAT XIII/2, 38—39 and in SVT 16 (1967), 244. He suggests wᵉhišlîk is a spelling or reading error for the Aramaic wᵉhašlêaḥ. In the Aramaic šlḥ would mean to "peel off" ("entrinden"). Cf. also Allen, op. cit., 47 footnote 7.

[16] Keller, op. cit., 111.

passage (6a—7b) one could indicate the following, even closer links: firstly 6b links up with 6a. At šinnâw there is a pronominal reiteration of gôj in 6a. Like the second part of stich 6a, 6b is a nominal clause describing the gôj. 7a and 7b are linked primarily with each other since they describe the devastating onslaught of the gôj on the vines and fig trees. In 6a the locusts are compared with a mighty hostile army, and in 6b their teeth are hyperbolically compared with a lion's. Everything contributes to underscore the devastating impact of these locusts.

As far as ornamentation is concerned, the alliteration in 6b, 7a and 7b is striking: šinnâw šinnê-6b; šam . . . leˢšāmmā-7a; ḥaśop ḥaśapah-7b. Probably this too serves to emphasize the destruction. Although views differ on the *metre* of 1 5—7, most of the stichs have a 3+2 metre.[17]

The *Gattung* of this strophe will be discussed when we deal with 1 5—14 in its entirety.

There are no *traditions* in the proper sense of the word, yet one could cite a few standard motifs: gôj . . . ˤaṣûm is a stereotyped expression[18] developed further in 2 2 and 5. Here it is used to indicate the awesome magnitude of the plague of locusts. The gæpæn and teˢenā (7a) often symbolize peace, tranquillity, prosperity and salvation.[19] Here in 1 5—7 these symbols are used ironically, for instead of signifying wellbeing, they are associated with the summons to lament.

We can *sum up* 1 5—7 as follows: 5a contains a vehement *summons to lament* (see detailed discussion below), which is substantiated in 5b and further elaborated in 6a—7b. The people are deprived of the symbols of prosperity and peace, a weighty reason for the lament. The catastrophe strikes mainly the šikkôrîm and the šotê jajin. The first person singular suffixes in 6a (ˀărṣî) and 7a (găpnî, teˢenatî) indicate that the speaker here is Yahweh. Hence it is actually his land, his vineyards and his figtrees that are stricken. What effects the people affects Yahweh as well, implying his involvement with human suffering: he is not merely a spectator.

---

[17] Cf. Bewer, op. cit., 77; Allen, op. cit., 46; Robinson, op. cit., 59.
[18] Cf. e.g. Gen 18 18; Dtn 9 14; 26 5; Mi 4 7; Dan 11 25.
[19] Cf. e.g. I Reg 5 5; II Reg 18 31; Hos 2 12; Mi 4 4; Jer 5 17; Sach 3 10; Cant 2 13.

(3) 1 8–10

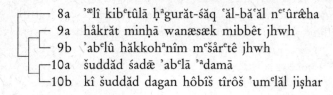

8a   ʾælî kibᵉtûlā ḫᵃgurăt-śăq ᶜăl-băᶜăl nᵉᶜûræ̂ha
9a   håkrăt minḥā wanæsæk mibbêt jhwh
9b   ʾabᵉlû hăkkohᵃnîm mᵉšårᵉtê jhwh
10a šuddăd śadæ̂ ʾabᵉlā ʾᵃdamā
10b kî šuddăd dagan hôbîš tîrôš ʾumᵉlăl jiṣhar

This strophe is again introduced by an imperative (8: ʾælî). It is not clear to whom this summons is addressed, but the feminine singular of the imperative would suggest that it is directed to the nation as a whole. By contrast with the previous strophe, Yahweh is referred to in the third person.

The *structure* of the strophe is as follows: 10a and 10b are interlinked by the emphatic kî. 10b thus specifies and accentuates 10a. In 10a the fields are personified. Striking too are the passive forms in 10a (šuddăd) and 10b (šuddăd, ʾumᵉlăl) as is the alliteration in both verses (10a, šuddăd śadæ̂ and 10b hôbîš tîrôš). The alliteration most likely serves to accentuate the "gesteigerte Leidenschaft".[20]

9a and 9b are similarly interlinked, particularly as regards content. Both stichs describe the breakdown of cultic life. Verse 9a deals more specifically with the bêt jhwh, whereas 9b concerns the mᵉšårᵉtê jhwh.

Note the lexeme from the previous strophe recurring in 9a (min + krt). In 5b we heard of the ᶜasîs "cut off" from the mouths of the wine drinkers; here the house of the Lord is deprived of offerings. The lexeme recurrence indicates progression.

Lines 10a/10b link up with 9a/9b, the connection being apparent particularly in the marked lexeme reiteration ʾabᵉlû – 9b, ʾabᵉlā – 10a.

Stich 8 has an overarching logical connection. The *tertium comparationis* of the image here is that of a virgin who in some *unforeseen* way loses her lover before the wedding,[21] so that instead of bridal apparel she has to put on mourning.

---

[20] Wolff, BKAT XIV/2, 36. E. D. Mallon, A stylistic analysis of Joel 1:10–12, CBQ 45 (1983), 543, describes hôbîš tîrôš as a vocalic chiasm.

[21] Cf. Wolff, BKAT XIV/2, 34–35. Rudolph, KAT XIII/2, 44–45; Allen, op. cit., 52–53; Thompson, IB 6, 739; Kapelrud's view op. cit., 32, "The phrasing of v. 8 may have been a formula which originally referred to the virgin, whose mourning for her lover, her brother, and Baal was prototypal for all Canaanites in ancient times, the 'Virgin Anat's' mourning for the deceased Baal", (cf. also Bič, op. cit., 22–24 and Keller, op. cit., 113) is unacceptable. Cf. Wolff, BKAT XIV/2, 34 and Rudolph, KAT XIII/2, 44–45.

Here too the *metre* does not yield dramatic results,[22] although G. A. Smith[23] points out an important feature: "The longer lines into which Hebrew parallelism tends to run are replaced by a rapid series of short, heavy phrases, falling like blows . . . (i. e. v. 10, W.S.P.) Joel loads his clauses with the most leaden letters he can find, and drops them in quick succession, repeating the same heavy word again and again, as if he would stun the careless people into some sense of the bare, brutal weight of the calamity which has befallen them."

The strophe does not contain any *traditions*, although 10b uses a conventional formula to indicate the principal agricultural products of Palestine, namely dagan, tîrôš, jiṣhar.[24]

These crops, a sign and symbol of Yahweh's blessing and presence, are devastated, indicating that the harmony between Yahweh and his people has been disturbed.[25]

In this strophe the summons is continued (8): this time the entire nation is involved and the crisis is illustrated with a vivid image. The crisis is particularly apparent in two areas — the cultus (9a/9b) and agriculture (10a/10b). The minḥā and næsæk,[26] the daily morning and evening offerings, have been taken away from the bêt jhwh; the priestly ministry is disrupted.[27]

---

[22] Cf. Allen, op. cit., 47; Robinson, op. cit., 59; Bewer, op. cit., 80.

[23] As quoted by Bewer, op. cit., 81.

[24] Cf. e.g. also Dtn 7 13; 11 14; 28 51; Hos 2 8 (11); Ps 104 15ff.

[25] Allen, op. cit., 54.

[26] Here the dilemma regarding the dating of the book emerges clearly. Some scholars maintain that minḥā wanæsæk occurs in this combination only in postexilic texts and use this as an argument for a postexilic dating. Cf. e. g. Wolff, BKAT XIV/2, 36; Ch. Chary, Les Prophètes et le Culte à partir de l'exil, (Bibliothèque de Théologie III/III), 1955, 198ff.; H. Holzinger, ZAW 9 (1889), 108. Others believe that this terminology does not constitute grounds for a postexilic dating. (Cf. Rudolph, KAT XIII/2, 45; Kapelrud, op. cit., 37).

[27] Wolff, BKAT XIV/2, 36, Chary, op. cit., 197 and Holzinger, op. cit., 101ff. use the expressions bêt jhwh and mᵉšārᵉtê jhwh to demonstrate the postexilic origin of Joel, whereas Kapelrud, op. cit., 45, Bič, op. cit., 26—27, Rudolph, KAT XIII/2, 45, are not swayed by these arguments. It is an inescapable problem that the dating of a book often coincides with an exegete's preconceptions, and that it then determines his interpretation of that book. Naturally correct dating is a major component of the hermeneutic process, but when a dating based on presuppositions, determines the subjective slant of the entire exegetic process one has to call for caution. No matter how important dating may be, extraneous data may not be imported into the text. The data in the text must be dealt with circumspectly. When it comes to Joel one must also enquire whether textual data permit any (exact) dating, and whether such a dating is indispensable for interpreting the book.

That is to say, the daily communion with Yahweh has grinded to a virtual standstill. It is worth noting — and the formal structure underscores the point — that the cultus and agriculture are not two distinct affairs, but interrelate closely. Service of Yahweh and the crops of the fields are not in separate compartments, so that the catastrophe that struck the harvest (locusts) directly influences the conduct of cultic worship.

(4) 1 11a—12c

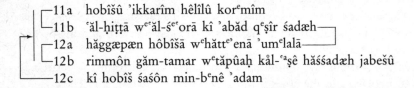

Like its predecessors, this strophe starts with an imperative (hobîšû).[28] The specific form (Hifil, bwš) is probably used for the sake of an assonance with the Hifil of jbš in 10b.[29] Line 11a, which manifests a formal parallelism, addresses the agriculturists, in particular the viticulturists.[30] 11b links up with 11a: the double ʿăl indicates what should be lamented, and kî gives the actual reason. Hence in this respect 11a/11b strongly resembles 5a/5b, 6a. Lines 12a and 12b are connected mainly by their content. The different fruit trees are enumerated one after another in sequence.[31] Verses 12a and

---

[28] hobîšu and hêlîlu can in fact be interpreted as either perfects or imperatives. On the strength of the overall structure of this pericope, and on the analogy of verses 5, 8a and 13 the imperatives are to be preferred (cf. W. Baumgartner, Joel 1 und 2, (BZAW 34), 1920; Thompson, IB 6, 739; Sellin, op. cit., 153; D. Deden, De kleine profeten, (BOT), 1953, 94; Robinson, op. cit., 59; Wolff, BKAT XIV/2, 21 footnote 11; Rudolph, KAT XIII/2, 39 footnote 11a; Allen, op. cit., 47, footnote 10). Interestingly the LXX renders the first words as a perfect and the second as an imperative, but some exegetes render both these forms with a perfect. Sometimes the choice seems to be determined by the way the pericope is demarcated (cf. D. W. Nowack, op. cit., 92; Kapelrud, op. cit., 41; Keller, op. cit., 114; Bewer, op. cit., 82 says about v. 11: "The prophet need not exhort them by an imperative call to be disappointed, he describes their grief and consternation").

[29] T. H. Robinson, op. cit., 59.

[30] There is really no contextual evidence for H. Gese, Kleine Beiträge zum Verständnis des Amosbuches, VT 12 (1962), 433, to maintain that ʾikkarîm in conjunction with korᵉmîm should be understood as "Landarbeiter".

[31] Cf. the various commentaries ad loc. for a discussion of the different trees.

12b further substantiate the summons in 11a and thus link up with the preceding lines. Whereas 11b concerns the cereal crop, 12a/12b deals with the fruit crop.

Contrary to the view of T. Frankfort,[32] 12c should not be seen as a motivative clause, for if that were the case it would have to be linked directly with 12a/12b. In fact it is a resumé of the entire strophe[33] and interpreters are virtually unanimous in regarding kî as an affirmative kî[34]. For this reason 12c links overarchingly with 11a—12b.

Rudolph[35] regards 12c as the concluding line of the whole of 1 5—12, maintaining that bᵉnê ʾadam is a general concept embracing all the different parties addressed from verse 5 onwards. Rudolph's opinion is probably determined by the fact that he starts a new pericope at 1 13, although there are weighty reasons why this should not be done.[36] 1 13 merely introduces a new strophe. The bᵉnê ʾadam should not be seen as a collective term for all the parties addressed as from verse 5, but should be interpreted literally as referring to the agriculturists in 1 10—12.

The *metre* does not help substantially to determine the structure.[37]

Word-play and *lexeme repetition* feature prominently in this strophe. In the first place there are lexemes repeated from and word-play on the *strophe immediately preceding* this one. We have referred to the hôbîš (10b) and hobîšû (11a), a word-play elaborated further in 12a (hôbîšā), 12b (jabᵉšû) and 12c (hobîš). The word-play between the two stems bwš and jbš displays a chiastic structure in this strophe:

11a	hobîšû	(bwš)
12a	hôbîša	(jbš)
12b	jabešû	(jbš)
12c	hobîš	(bwš)

It would seem as if the meanings of bwš and jbš more or less fuse in *12c*. The artistry of the repetition and word-play helps to stress the magnitude and gravity of the catastrophe.

---

[32] Le מִי de Joël I 12, VT 10 (1960), 445—448.

[33] Keller, op. cit., 114: "Le dernier vers résume ce qui précède …". Cf. also Allen, op. cit., 55, footnote 4.

[34] Thompson, IB 6, 740; Deden, op. cit., 94; Bewer, op. cit., 83; Wolff, BKAT XIV/2, 37; Rudolph, KAT XIII/2, 43.

[35] Op. cit., 46.

[36] Cf. discussion above.

[37] Cf. e.g. Allen, op. cit., 47 and Robinson, op. cit., 59.

Further lexeme repetitions may be found in 10b (ʾumᵉlăl) and 12a (ʾumᵉlalā), as well as śadæh (11b), and śadæh (12b) with śadæ (10a). Note that the lexemes repeated in this strophe (1 11—12) are taken exclusively from the second part (10a/10b) — the so-called agricultural section (see structure) — of the previous strophe (1 8—10).[38]

In addition this strophe repeats some lexemes from strophe 1 5—7: hêlîlû (11a) and hêlilû (5a). The substantion for the summons in these two strophes is analogous: ʿăl + kî (cf. 5a/5b, 6 with 11b). Other lexeme recurrences are haggæpæn and tᵉʾenā (12a) from 7a.

By and large we would agree that the repetition of previously used verbs (and other words) "adds to the mournful effect of this verse".[39] The repetitions have an accentuating, climactic effect.

Note for instance, how the repetition of the preposition min adds to this *Steigerung*: the catastrophe means that the wine drinkers are deprived of their wine (mippêkæm, 5b); that offerings are no longer brought in the house of the Lord (mibbêt jhwh — 9a); it also means that the people are deprived of all joy (min⁻bᵉnê ʾadam, 12c).

Hence each successive strophe substantiates the *Aufruf* more firmly. The catastrophe has an impact on the wine drinkers (1 5—7), on agriculture and cultic life (1 8—10), but in 1 11—12 it is a matter of "nackte Existenz",[40] of people's staple food and natural means of survival that have been destroyed. The farmers are called to be "confounded" (11a), because the cereal (11b) and fruit crops have been entirely destroyed (12b). The upshot is that there is no longer any cause for joy (12c).

(5) 1 13a—14c

13a ḥigᵉrû wᵉsipᵉdû hăkohᵃnîm hêlîlû mᵉšărtê mizbeăḥ
13b boʾû lînû băśśăqqîm mᵉšărtê ʾælohaj
13c kî nimnăʿ mibbêt ʾælohêkæm minḥā wanasæk
14a qaddᵉšû-ṣôm qirᵉʾû ʿaṣarā
14b ʾisᵉpû zᵉqenîm kol jošᵉbê haʾaræṣ
14c bêt jhwh ʾælohêkæm wᵉzăʾᵃqû ʾæl-jhwh

---

[38] Cf. discussion above where we show that the next strophe, 1 13—14 repeats lexemes from the first part (8—9) of strophe 1 8—10. In a sense these strophes, 1 8—10; 1 11—12 and 1 13—14 therefore display a chiastic structure. Contra Mallon, CBQ 45 (1983), 537—548 who regards 1 10—12 as a unity.

[39] Thompson, IB 6, 740.

[40] Rudolph, KAT XIII/2, 45.

We have mentioned that several exegetes would like to have a new peri-cope start at 1 13.[41] The fact is that 1 13a—14c constitutes a section or strophe of the pericope 1 2—14 in view of the strong *formal* resemblances to the preceding strophes. It is introduced by imperatives which are again fol-lowed by a substantiation (kî, 13c). In addition there are striking lexeme repetitions from the preceding strophes: koh³nîm (13a) — 9b; hêlîlû (13a) — 5a, 11a; mᵉšårtê 'ᵅlohaj (13b); mᵉšårᵉtê jhwh (9b); šăqqîm (13b), śaq (8a). 13c repeats 9a virtually verbatim, apart from the substitution of håkrăt for nimnă', and jhwh for 'ᵅlohaj. The word sequence also differs slightly.

It is remarkable that most of the lexemes are repeated from the *first part* of strophe 1 8—10, namely from 1 8—9. We have already mentioned that 1 11—12 contains a conspicuous number of lexeme recurrences from the latter part of 1 8—10 (1 10). Hence there appears to be a chiastic corre-spondence between 1 8—10; 1, 11—12 and 1 13—14.

1 8—10	*General invocation:*	
	— *priestly service*/cultus disrupted	(a)
	— *Agriculture* disrupted	(b)
1 11—12	Summoning *farmers*	(b)
1 13—14	Summoning *priests*	(a)

This integration with the preceding strophes lends additional force to the argument against starting a new pericope at 1 13. Wolff also argues plausibly that the *Gattung* of the passage reaches its actual climax and pur-pose in this final strophe.[42]

There are no significant *text-critical* emendations to be made to this strophe.[43]

As for the *structure* of 1 13a—14c, the following: 13a links up with 13b. Both stichs abound in imperatives: ḥigᵉrû, hêlîlû-13a; bo'û, lînû-13b; and in both, these imperatives are addressed to the priests: hăkoh³nîm, mᵉ—sårtê mizbeăḥ 13a; mᵉšårtê 'ᵅlohaj-13b.

Through the substantiating kî 13c is overarchingly linked with the preceding two strophes. Syntactically 14a, b and c are on a par, for once again there is a string of imperatives: qaddᵉšû, qirᵉ'u-14a; 'isᵉpû-14b; ză'ª-

---

[41] Cf. footnote 36 above.

[42] Wolff, BKAT XIV/2, 37. For a more detailed discussion cf. p. 25ff. below.

[43] There are no valid grounds for changing 'ᵅlohaj in 13b to 'ᵅlohîm on strength of the LXX. (Wolff, BKAT XIV/2, 21; Bewer, op. cit., 86, T. H. Robinson, op. cit., 59) or even to 'ᵅlohêkæm. (Rudolph, KAT XII/2, 39).

qû-14c. However, the first halfline of 14c contains no verb and depends syntactically on 14b — with which it forms a colon — so that one has to link the two.

The first half line of 14c designates the *place* where the people should assemble, and the second half line indicates the *purpose* of the gathering namely zǎʾᵃqû ʾæl-jhwh. One could regard 14b/c as a specification of 14a, so that Thompson is right in contending that the zǎʾᵃqû ʾælˑjhwh constitutes a climax.[44]

Once again the *metre* does not add much to the structure of the strophe,[45] nor are there any clear-cut *traditions*.

The *redaction history* of some of the strophes in this pericope warrants further comment. Although 13c could be a variant of 9a, one cannot maintain that it did not occur in its present position originally, nor can one simply omit it.[46] Repetitions of and play on words are common in Joel and are in fact used for emphasis.

To sum up, 13ab emphatically calls the priests to prayer and fasting in the temple. This is substantiated (13c) by once again citing the disruption of sacrificial worship. But the summons is not confined to the priests alone: the entire nation has to be summoned (14a/b), the real purpose of the gathering being to pray to Yahweh. The strophe is markedly theocentric, as is evident from the choice of words: (mᵉšårtê ʾælohaj-13b; mibbêt ʾælohêkæm-13c) and particularly from the climax (14c), where it is said that the gathering must culminate in a "Notschrei zu Jahwe". [47] Hence the fasting and sackcloth are in effect merely a means to an end, which is to pray to the Lord.

The various strophes or sections of the pericope are interlinked in a special way. We have referred to the formal correspondences and the many lexeme reiterations.

The interrelationship of sections may be depicted thus:

1 2— 4   General invocation
1 5— 7   Summons to drunkards
1 8—10   General invocation concerning disrupted priestly service and agriculture
1 11—12 Summons to farmers
1 13—14 Summons to priests.

---

44 Thompson, IB 6, 240.
45 Cf. Allen, op. cit., 55; Bewer, op. cit., 84; Robinson, op. cit., 59.
46 Cf. Bewer, ICC, 86. T. H. Robinson, 59 comments as follows: "13c stört nicht nur die metrische Symmetrie, sondern bringt auch einen unpassenden Gedanken hinein."
47 Rudolph, KAT XIII/2, 47.

The general invocation to the entire nation (1 2−4) would appear to be specified more closely in the respective strophes where the different elements of the population are addressed individually. In the composite section 1 5−14 one finds that 1 8−14 − on account of the aforementioned chiastic structure and numerous lexeme recurrences − probably constitutes an even closer unity. The structure of the pericope thus helps to affirm that the *entire nation* is being summoned.

For a meaningful appraisal of the theology of the pericope one would have to consider its *Gattung* as well. H. W. Wolff made a real contribution when be classified the *Gattung* of 1 5−14 as a *Aufruf zur Volksklage*.[48] The conventional elements of this *Gattung* are (*1*) imperatives (cf. 1 5, 8, 11, 13, 14), accompanied by (*2*) vocatives (1 5, 11, 13), and (*3*) substantiation of the *Aufruf*. The substantiation is introduced by either kî or ʿăl, and is stated as a fact by means of the perfect tense. There are eleven other Old Testament passages where structure and vocabulary are similar enough to permit us to speak of a *Gattung*. (See Isa 14 31; 23 1−14; 32 11−14; Jer 6 26; 25 34; 49 3; Ez 21 17; Zeph 1 11; Sach 11 2; see also II Sam 1 24). Wolff[49] regards the four strophes of 1 5−14 as "das schönste, gleichmäßig ausgebildete Beispiel" of the call for a national lament.

W. Janzen,[50] H.-P. Müller[51] and A. Baumann[52] adopted Wolff's term. As far back as 1920 W. Baumgartner[53] referred to 1 5−14 as an *Aufruf zur Klage* and distinguished the same conventional elements in the *Gattung* as Wolff did. Keller[54] speaks of "la proclamation d'un jeûne général à l'occasion d'une calamité nationale". Irsigler[55] defines the *Gattung* even more precisely when he calls 1 5−14 an "Aufruf zur rituellen Klagefeier an das Yahwevolk".

Naturally one's demarcation of the pericope will influence one's assessment of its *Gattung*. Thus Rudolph[56] deals with the *Gattung* of 1 13−14 as a separate unit which he describes as an "Aufforderung zum Fasten und Beten". But the two elements which he identifies should rather be seen as components of the call for a national lament.

---

[48] Cf. BKAT XIV/2, 23−24; Der Aufruf zur Volksklage, ZAW 76 (1964), 48−56.

[49] ZAW 76 (1964), 54.

[50] W. Janzen, Morning cry and woe oracle, (BZAW 125), 89.

[51] Prophetie und Apokalyptik bei Joel, Theologia Viatorum 10 (1965/6), 234.

[52] ילל II/1 in ThWAT Band III/6−7, 641−643.

[53] (BZAW 34), 1920, 11.

[54] Op. cit., 110.

[55] Gottesgericht und Jahwetag, 1977, 278.

[56] KAT XIII/2, 46.

C. Hardmeier[57] also refuses to accept Wolff's idea, maintaining that one should distinguish between ritual mourning and a cultic lament. The former would be wholly profane, the latter should be viewed in a cultic context. Hardmeier claims that 1 5–13 is a ritual cry of mourning, whereas 1 14 is an *Aufruf zur Klagefeier*. Hence he regards 1 14 as a *Neueinsatz* within the larger whole of 1 2–20. The cry of mourning (1 5–13) is the substantiating background to the *Klagefeier* (1 14), with as its *Sitz im Leben* the profane chants of mourning rather than the cultic *Sitz* of the *Klagefeier*.

In reply to this one would have to point out that it is quite impossible to distinguish between the profane and the cultic in Joel. The original *Sitz im Leben* might well have differed, but as the two facets appear in Joel today they form an indissoluble unity, confirmed by the formal structure of the pericope. W. Baumgartner[58] aptly sums it up: "Die gemeinsame Form bindet V 5-14 zu einem Ganzen zusammen, das keinerlei Zerlegung oder Ausscheidung duldet."

The cry for a national lament, usually emanating from someone in authority,[59] is here used to bring home the gravity of the situation and to call the people to repentance.

The original *Sitz im Leben* — that is the crisis situation depicted here — most probably left its mark on the *Gattung*. The prophet was unable to address all the groups within the nation simultaneously, as witness the written form of the various strophes.[60]

The *redaction history* of this pericope ties in with the problems attending the redaction history of Joel as a whole.[61] As pointed out in the formal analysis, the pericope displays a logical cohesiveness strongly indicative of a single author.

On the basis of our exegesis so far, here are some guidelines to the *theology* of 1 2–14. Naturally the passage will ultimately have to be evaluated in the light of the theology of Joel as a whole.

The importance of the tidings and the comprehensiveness of the calamity are conveyed by the *Gattungen* (*Lehreröffnungsruf* and *Aufruf zur Klage*). The crisis involves the entire community. But the plague of locusts is not interpreted purely as a natural disaster, but as an event calling men to

---

[57] Texttheorie und biblische Exegese, 1978, 344–346.
[58] Op. cit., 12.
[59] Allen, op. cit., 11.
[60] Wolff, ZAW 76 (1964), 54; cf. Müller's (Theol. Viatorum 10 (1965/6), 234, footnote 12) comment.
[61] Cf. W. S. Prinsloo, NGTT XXIV (1983), 255–258.

repentance. In this crisis Yahweh is no *deus otiosus*. Because this is his land and his people he is implicated with them in the crisis. The agricultural calamity is not isolated: it hits *all* the people – neither wine drinkers nor priests escape it – and the *whole* of life: not only are the main crops of the fields devastated, but the daily communion with Yahweh suffers. Men have been deprived of their staple foods, but normal cultic life has also been suspended. Farming and religion are intimately linked. As shown in the discussion, these points are heavily accentuated, both by the climactic structure of the pericope and the chiastic correspondence between strophes; the climax is reached in the final strophe (1 13–14) where the call for a national lament achieves its real purpose.[62] Here not only the priests but the whole nation are called to repentance; more particularly – and this is the climax – these cultic devotions must culminate in supplications to God. The national lament about the crisis achieves its climax and true purpose in the cry of distress to Yahweh. Hence especially the final strophe is theocentric.

The pericope reveals an *inclusio* in the all but identical 1 2 (šimᵉᶜû) and 1 14b (ʾisᵉpu zᵉqenîm), although one can discern a progression between them. Whereas 1 2 is still summons to take heed of the extraordinary character of the event, 1 14b is an invocation to turn to Yahweh because of it.

Hence the plague of locusts is a sign pointing the way to Yahweh.

---

[62] Wolff, BKAT XIV/2, 37.

IV. 1 15–20

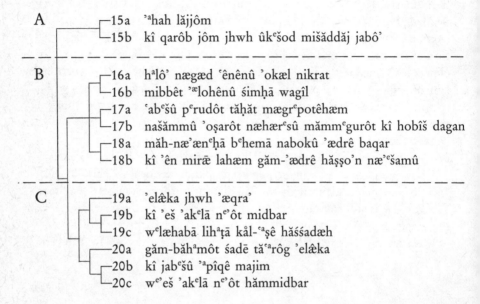

A
   ┌─15a ʾᵃhah lǎjjôm
   └─15b kî qarôb jôm jhwh ûkᵉšod mišǎddǎj jabôʾ

B
   ┌─16a hᵃlôʾ nægæd ᶜênênû ʾokæl nikrat
   └─16b mibbêt ʾᵅlohênû śimḫā wagîl
   ┌─17a ᶜabᵉšû pᵉrudôt tǎḫǎt mægrᵉpotêhæm
   └─17b našǎmmû ʾoṣarôt næhærᵉsû mǎmmᵉgurôt kî hobîš dagan
   ┌─18a mǎh-næʾænᵉḫā bᵉhemā nabokû ʾædrê baqar
   └─18b kî ʾên mirǣ lahæm gǎm-ʾædrê hǎṣṣoʾn næʾᵉšamû

C
   ┌─19a ʾelǽka jhwh ʾæqraʾ
   ├─19b kî ʾeš ʾakᵉlā nᵉʾôt midbar
   └─19c wᵉlæhabā lihᵃṭā kål-ᶜᵃṣê hǎśśadæh
   ┌─20a gǎm-bǎhᵃmôt śadē tǎᶜᵃrôg ʾelǽka
   ┌─20b kî jabᵉšû ʾᵃpîqê majim
   └─20c wᵉᵉš ʾakᵉlā nᵉʾôt hǎmmidbar

The new pericope is introduced by a stereotyped cry, ʾᵃhah. Here the dominant feature of the previous pericopes, namely strophes introduced by imperatives, is absent. Thematically too it introduces a new element, the Yom Yahweh. 1 15–20 is *demarcated* from the next pericope which also starts with a conventional introductory formula at 2 1.

A few text-critical[1] problems need to be mentioned. W. Rudolph[2] calls 1 17 the "eigentliche crux des Joelbuchs", and M. Sprengling[3] writes about it thus: "This verse in the book of Joel is well known to every serious student of Hebrew"(!). The problem lies in the fact that three of the four words in 17a are *hapax legomena*. One could ask whether this is in fact a text-critical problem and whether these words, although unknown to us, might not have been familiar to the original audience. Although the scores

---

[1] Cf. the text-critical apparatus in BHS and BHK³.
[2] SVT 16 (1967), 244.
[3] M. Sprengling, Joel 1,17, JBL 38 (1919), 129.

of proposed solutions represent commendable efforts,[4] they have merely added to the confusion rather than simplified matters. An honest exegete will have to acknowledge that he is faced with an insoluble problem.[5] The nearest one can come to a solution is to note the close syntactic link between 17a and 17b: ʿabᵉṣû and našămmû are both third person singular verbs, whilst the subjects, pᵉrudôt (17a) and ʾoṣarôt (17b) are both feminine plural. Since 17b concerns the devastation of the cereal crop it seems likely that 17a refers to the same thing.

18b also calls for comment. There is a strong tendency to change næʾᵉšamû (Nifal of ʾšm, "to become punishable")[6] to našămmû (Nifal of šmm, "to be destroyed") on the strength of the LXX. The arguments for such a change are not, however, entirely convincing.[7] A change cannot be introduced solely on the strength of the LXX. The næʾᵉšamû may be retained as it stands and taken to mean that everyone, hence the sheep as well, are imperilled by the catastrophe and hence must pay a price.[8]

The structure of 1 15–20 is as follows. The pericope comprises three sections: (1) 15a/b, the *Schreckenruf* and its substantiation; (2) 16a–18b, introduced by a rhetorical question and first person plural forms, and (3) 19a–20c which displays an exquisitely finished microstructure of its own.

The various stichs are connected as follows: 15a at once hits one in the eye because of its unusual metre. The cry, ʾᵃhah in 15a is substantiated in 15b. The lăjjôm is the so-called pregnant dative,[9] stressing the imminence of the Yom. This day is qarôb and is coming (jabô' – imperfect). The kᵉ (kᵉšod) is the so-called *kaf-veritatis*,[10] underscoring the full reality of the Yom. As for ornamentation, 15b contains a remarkable assonance, ûkᵉšod

---

[4] For a detailed discussion of the problem and an outline of the various possibilities cf. E. Nestle, Miscellen I. Joel 1, 17, ZAW 20 (1900), 164–165; M. Sprengling, JBL 38 (1919), 129–141; W. Rudolph, SVT 16 (1967), 244–250; Rudolph, KAT XIII/2, 39–40; Wolff, BKAT XIV/2, 22; Kapelrud, op. cit., 65–66; Bewer, op. cit., 91 writes about this text: "V¹⁷ᵃ must therefore not be corrected but omitted."

[5] After examining the different exegetical possibilities Miloš Bič, op. cit., 44 rightly observes: "Diese Übersicht zeigt, wie schwer, ja geradezu unmöglich es ist, den eigentlichen Sinn dieser Verse zu erfassen."

[6] Cf. e.g. Wolff, BKAT XIV/2, 22; Bewer, op. cit., 91–92; Sellin, op. cit., 156; Robinson, op. cit., 16; Thompson, IB 6, 742. The argument is that this text contains the only instance of the Nifal ʾšm, and that it is the only one to apply to animals. There is however insufficient external evidence to warrant the change. Besides, šmm never applies to animals.

[7] Cf. Commentaries ad loc.

[8] Cf. Kapelrud, op. cit., 67–68; also Keller, op. cit., 118 footnote 1.

[9] Rudolph, KAT XIII/2, 47; cf. also Keller, op. cit., 116.

[10] Deden, op. cit., 96.

mišaddăj. This name, used as a designation for Yahweh mainly in the patriarchal history,[11] is directly linked with šod, that is destruction, through
the use of assonance,[12] which therefore signifies that this jôm is a day of
devastation and terror.

Kapelrud rightly maintains: "Yahweh's Day is near, and it shall appear
as a day of woe. This, in Joel, is the main point."[13] Syntactically 16a and
16b constitute a unit: 16b contains no verb, but the nikrat of 16a is assumed. There is moreover a correlation as regards the first person plural
suffixes (ʿênênû, 16a; ʾælohênu, 16b). Hence 16b qualifies 16a, in that it is a
matter of the disruption of *cultic communion* with Yahweh ("our God").
The rhetorical question with which 16a opens (hᵃlôʾ) stresses the inescapability of the situation. The expression nægæd ʿênênû is accentuated by its
prominent position in the sentence:[14] the people perceive the catastrophe,
but are helpless in the face of it.

As shown earlier, 17a and 17b are linked by virtue of the correlating
third person plural verbs (ʿabᵉšû, 17a; našămmu, næhærᵉsû, 17b) and the
feminine plural nouns (pᵉrudôt, 17a; ʾoṣarôt and mămmᵉgurôt, 17b). Lines
17a and 17b depict the catastrophe in *agricultural* terms.

18a and 18b are linked up through the motivative kî. In 18b there is a
resumption of bᵉhemā and ʾædrê baqar by means of the third person plural
suffix (lahæm). There is also lexeme repetition between 18a and 18b
(ʾædrê), and in addition both stichs contain third person plural Nifal perfect
forms (næʾænᵉḥā, nabokû, 18a; næʾᵉšamû, 18b). The măh, which is given
syntactic prominence in 18a,[15] and the personification of the animals both
heighten the dramatic effect of this description of the crisis, as does the assonance in 18a (nabokû ... baqar).

The three stich sections, 16a/b, 17a/b and 18a/b, are all interlinked at
the same level, chiefly as regards content — the crisis situation, which is
viewed from three different angles: the cultus (16a/b), agriculture (17a/b),
and even the animals (18a/b) all of which are in dire straits. This indicates
not only the comprehensive character of the calamity, but also that the different aspects of society are not to be separated and are intimately linked.
The structure of the final section of this pericope (1 19—20) is fascinating.

---

[11] Gen 17 1; 43 14; 49 25; cf. also Ex 6 3; Num 24 4; Ps 68 14 (15); 91 1.

[12] Hence it is not a case of finding the original meaning of šaddaj or its correct etymology —
    both highly controversial points in themselves — but of the function of the assonance.

[13] Kapelrud, op. cit., 58.

[14] Thompson, IB 6, 741.

[15] Cf. Kapelrud, op. cit., 67.

Firstly, it is set apart from the previous section in that the first person plural of the latter now becomes a first person singular ('æqra'). Also Yahweh is no longer the subject of discussion but is addressed directly (19a). The deliberate positioning of 'elæka in the construction of the sentence accentuates the fact that these words are addressed to Yahweh. 19b is connected with 19a by the causal kî, yet 19b links up primarily with 19c because the motive for the cry to Yahweh is continued in 19c (note the waw copula here). 20a, b and c show considerable symmetry with 19a, b and c: In 20a the person addressed is still Yahweh, but the subject now is băhªmôt.[16] The emphatic găm in 20a indicates that not just the prophet but even the beasts are calling out to Yahweh. The causal kî links 20b with the preceding 20a, but on the same grounds cited for 19b/c, 20b/c have a prior connection. Structurally, therefore, 19a, b and c and 20a, b and c are symmetrical. We can illustrate it thus:

19a:	'elæka	20a:	găm . . . 'elæka
19b:	kî	20b:	kî
19c:	wᵉ	20c:	wᵉ

Note also the marked repetition of 19b in 20c,[17] the sole difference being that kî 'eš 'akᵉlā nᵉ'ôt midbar occurs in the first column of the substantiation in verse 19, whereas in verse 20 it occurs in the second column:

```
┌─19a   kî 'eš . . .
└─19c
┌─20b
└─20c   kî 'eš . . .
```

This gives the substantiation an *inclusio*, a finishing touch enhancing its perfection. The refrain stresses the focal issue of this emergency, namely a scorching drought. The symmetrical structure of 19a, b and c and 20a, b and c vividly illustrates that man and beast alike suffer from this catastrophe and, so to speak, address a common cry of distress to Yahweh.[18] The use of

---

[16] The apparent contradiction namely that the noun (băhᵉmôt) is plural although the verb tăʿªrôg) is singular — is not uncommon and does not warrant text-critical emendation (cf. Keller, op. cit., 119, footnote 1.) The singular verb implies that the multitude consists of "pièces individuelles" (Keller, ibid.).

[17] J. A. Thompson, Repetition in the prophecy of Joel, 1974, 107.

[18] H. Frey, Das Buch der Kirche in der Weltwende, (BAT 24), 1948, 210.

verb forms in this section is significant:[19] in the prayer to Yahweh the *imperfect* is used ('æqra', 19a; tă'ªrôg, 20a); in the description of the prevailing crisis *the perfect* is used ('ak°lā, 19b; lih'ªṭā, 19c; jab°šû, 20b; 'ak°lā, 20c). This reflects the polarity between the crisis situation and the prayer addressed to Yahweh.

The *metre* does not tell us much about the structure. At most one can say that it is erratic.[20]

The three sections of this pericope (15a/b; 16—18; 19—20) interrelate as follows: It would seem that C shows similarities to, but also a climactic progression on B. Formally the two sections are alike in the prominence of the causal kî (17b, 18b, 19b, 20b.) Thematically too they are linked in that the desperate situation of the animals features in both. There is also a lexeme repetition (b°hemā, 18a; băh'ªmôt, 20a). In C the first person plural intensifies to the first person singular. One could also posit a *Steigerung* as regards *Gattung* (see below). For all these reasons we can connect B and C, whilst A logically links up overarchingly with both B and C:

```
┌──(15a/b)   A
│ ┌─(16—18)  B
└─┤
  └─(19—20)  C
```

B and C define more precisely and substantiate the announcement that the Yom Yahweh is near. In B the crisis in the cultus, in agriculture and stock farming is given as the reason. C takes matters further, describing the common cry of distress directed to Yahweh by man and beast because of this crisis.

The relation between this pericope and the preceding[21] (1 2—14) and the next one (2 1—11) also has to be noted. The lexeme reiteration from the preceding pericope is at once obvious: the stem krt, so prominent in 1 2—14 (cf. 5b and 9a) is once more in evidence in 16a. In 16a/b one finds krt in conjunction with bêt 'ælohênû. 9a is virtually identical: håkrăt minḥā wanæsæk mibbêt jhwh. The expression mibbêt jhwh also occurs in 14a. We have mentioned that the stems bwš and jbš play a significant role in 1 2—14 (especially in the third and fourth strophes). This *Stichwort* recurs in 20b (jab°šu). Thus 17b, kî hobîš dagan, is very like 10b: kî šuddad. We have

---

[19] Cf. Keller, op. cit., 118.

[20] Cf. Allen, op. cit., 56/57; Bewer, op. cit., 87/88; Robinson, op. cit., 61; Keller, op. cit., 115.

[21] Cf. M. Plath, Joel 1 15—20, ZAW 47 (1929), 159—160.

already referred to the alliteration in 10a (šuddad śadæ) and the recurrence of śadæh in 11b and 12b. In 1 15—20 śadæh is repeated in 19c and 20a. More than that, the assonance on šuddad reaches a climax with kešod mišaddaj in 15b, where the devastation is linked with Yahweh's ancient name from patriarchal history. The progression between the two pericopes is discernible at the level of vocabulary as well: zăʾaqû ʾæl-jhwh (1 14c, a *summons* to cry to Yahweh) progresses to ʾelȅka jhwh ʾæqraʾ (19a) and tăʿarôg ʾelȅka (20a), hence to actual prayer to Yahweh.

If we are to venture some provisional comments on the relation between 1 2—14 and 1 15—20 as manifested mainly in vocabulary, recurrent lexemes and assonance, the following points can be made:

The portents associated with the impending Yom Yahweh (1 15—20) are related to and described by analogy with the catastrophe accompanying the plague of locusts (1 2—14). From this we conclude that the plague of locusts and all that went with it are portents of the Yom Yahweh.

If we relate the Yom Yahweh in 1 15 to Yahweh's punitive action, one could call the plague of locusts "ein Handeln Jahwes".[22] Irsigler[23] rightly claims that the kî in 15 relates the formula in a causal and explicative way to the summons to lament in 1 5—14. Hence this summons is not an isolated formula. Within the structure of 1 2—20 the purpose of the conventional formula in 1 15a is to interpret the crisis (locusts, drought) as portent of the even greater calamity of the Yom Yahweh.[24]

There is no consensus about the *Gattung* of 1 15—20: Kapelrud[25] regards 1 16—18 as a lament, and 19—20 as a "personal address to Yahweh in the style of an individual psalm of lamentation". Allen[26] calls 1 15—18 a descriptive lament on the strength of its first person plural forms, but observes that there are third person references in 1 15. On the strength of these he claims that 1 15—18 "represent a transition from the description of the call of lament into the description to be found in an actual psalm of lament".[27] When it comes to 1 19—20 he is again unsure. "The first part reads like an individual lament which is marked by a first singular subject; otherwise the piece could be a communal lament, which like this one is characterized by address, petition and description."[28] W. Rudolph[29] regards 1

---

[22] E. Kutsch, Heuschreckenplage und Tag Jahwes in Joel 1 und 2, TZ 18/2 (1962), 82.
[23] Irsigler, op. cit., 326.
[24] Irsigler, op. cit., 327.
[25] Kapelrud, op. cit., 5.
[26] Allen, op. cit., 59.
[27] Allen, ibid.
[28] Allen, op. cit., 63.   [29] Rudolph, KAT XIII/2, 47.

15—18 not as a prayer, but as a reason for fasting and prayer, although he concedes that 1 19—20 is a *Bittgebet*.[30] T. H. Robinson[31] considers 1 16—18 to be a lament, but he sees the prayer of lamentation as starting, not at 1 16, but at 1 19.

A. Weiser[32] regards the whole of 1 15—20 as a prayer of lamentation, whilst H. W. Wolff[33] feels that it should not be seen as an "ausgeführte" lament, but as one reflecting fragments of two different kinds of lamentation. From the plurals in 1 16 the first fragment may be identified as a collective lament; the second, Wolff maintains, is found in ʾelǻka jhwh ʾæqraʾ in 19a and may be termed an individual lament. H.-P. Müller[34] claims that 1 16—20 contains a description of crisis similar to those found in laments in the Psalter. By contrast with those collective laments, which usually concern enemies, here the catastrophe is caused by natural disaster.[35] The stereotyped formula in 15a, ʾªhah lăjjôm, could be called a summons to lamentation or cry of terror,[36] although the latter rarely features in lamentations.[37] From the foregoing it is evident that 1 15—20 does not fit into any of the conventional *Gattungen*. One could apply to it W. Richter's comment:[38] "Gattung ist also ein theoretisches Ergebnis der Wissenschaft; in der konkreten Literatur existieren nur die Formen." Although the author of this pericope uses conventional forms, he does so idiosyncratically to achieve his own ends. The cry of terror and elements of collective and individual lamentations, no less than the cry of distress addressed to Yahweh by man and beast, serve to stress the gravity and magnitude of the crisis. In this sense the *Gattung* of 1 15—20 reflects a *Steigerung* on the preceding pericope: the summons to a national lament is intensified to a real cry of distress to Yahweh. In other words, the summons is heeded.

The *tradition history* of this pericope offers much food for thought. 1 15b contains the tradition of the Yom Yahweh encountered in other pro-

---

[30] Rudolph, KAT XIII/2, 49.
[31] Robinson, op. cit., 61.
[32] Weiser, ATD 24/1, 110.
[33] Wolff, BKAT XIV/2, 24; Wolff writes further (24—25): "Beiden Fragmenten fehlen neben sonstigen Stücken vor allem die im normalen Klagelied Israel kaum entbehrlichen Elemente der Bitte und des Gelübdes, auch der Vertrauensaussage."
[34] Theologia Viatorum 10 (1965/66), 235.
[35] Ibid.
[36] Irsigler, op. cit., 327.
[37] Wolff, BKAT XIV/2, 25. Cf. also Jdc 6 22; 11 35, II Reg 3 10; 6 5; Jer 1 6.
[38] Exegese als Literaturwissenschaft, 1971, 132.

phetic writings as well.[39] The terminology of Joel 1 15 (cf. also 2 1; 4 14b) corresponds closely with that of Isa 13 6; Zeph 1 7, 14; Ez 30 2 and Ob 15.[40]

Joel is clearly using conventional terminology and a known tradition, one that is so familiar as to need no explanation to his hearers/readers.[41]

When it comes to the origin of the Yom Yahweh tradition, opinions differ widely. We would agree with M. *Saebø*,[42] that despite any number of conjecture and speculations we know virtually nothing about its origin.[43]

---

[39] For the expression Yom Yahweh, cf. Am 5 18—20; Zeph 1 7, 14; Mal 3 23; Ez 13 15; Isa 13 6, 9; Ob 15. Variations and amplifications of this expression occur in several places in prophetic literature. One could argue that the point arises frequently even if it is not mentioned by name.

[40] From this one could infer that Joel should be given at least a post-exilic dating.

[41] Cf. G. von Rad, The origin of the concept of the Day of Yahweh, JSS IV (1959), 99: "It is evident from the way in which Joel pictures the distress that he is dependent on traditional, that is, more or less conventional, prophetic concepts; that is, on concepts which he applies only secondary to the actual locust plague."

[42] יום II—VI, ThWAT Band III/6—7, 1980, 583.

[43] The proposed solution usually depends on the presuppositions of the particular exegete. From the vast body of literature we cite some of the more important scholars: H. Gressmann, Der Ursprung der israelitisch-jüdischen Eschatologie, 1905, 8 ff. traces the origin of the Yom Yahweh in a nature-mythological day of salvation and doom; S. Mowinckel, Psalmenstudien (Buch I—II), 1961, 245 associates the origin of the Yom with the Enthronement feast. As one might expect, A. S. Kapelrud writes (op. cit., 55): "The conception of Yahweh's Day seems to have belonged to the cult and has not originated from some identical historic event or other". This is also the view of G. W. Ahlström, Joel and the temple cult of Jerusalem, (SVT XXI), 1971, 64 ff. Cf. also J. Lindblom in review of H. W. Wolff's commentary on Joel, ThLZ 90 (1965), 424; L. Černy, The day of Yahweh and some relevant problems 1948, 103 by and large accepts a cultic background. He traces the ideological sources of the Yom in the psychology of nomadic people. This psychological attitude he calls corporate personality. H. Gese, Geschichtliches Denken im Alten Orient und im Alten Testament, ZThK 55 (1958), 44 refers to the ". . . wohl aus dem Kult stammende Vorstellung vom Tage Jahwes." Gerhard von Rad, The origin of the concept of the Day of Yahweh, JSS V (1959), 97—108 adopted a widely influential viewpoint, namely that the Yom originated from the Holy War tradition ("tradition of the holy wars of Yahweh"). Cf. e. g. K. D. Schunck, Strukturlinien in der Entwicklung der Vorstellung vom Tag Jahwes, VT14 (1964), 319—330; cf. also K. D. Schunck, Die Eschatologie der Propheten des Alten Testaments und ihre Wandlung in exilisch-nachexilischer Zeit, SVT XXVI, 1974, 121 ff.; P. D. Miller, The divine council and the prophetic call to war, VT18 (1968), 100—107, claims that apart from the Holy War tradition certain other elements must be considered when one discusses the Yom. He maintains that the "divine council participates as a cosmic or heavenly army in the eschatological wars of Yahweh, those military activities associated with the day of Yahweh . . ." (100—101). Cf. M. Weippert, "Heiliger Krieg" in Israel und Assyrien. Kritische Anmerkungen zu Gerhard von Rads Konzept des "Heiligen Krieges" im Alten Israel, ZAW 84 (1972), 460—493. Hans-Martin Lutz, Jahwe, Jerusalem und die Völker

Even if the origin of the tradition could be established beyond all doubt it is questionable whether it would cast any light on the way it is used in Joel. The Yom Yahweh assumes many different meanings among the different prophets, yet overall one could say that it forms part of the eschatology of Israel[44] and that it helps in a very real way to give prophetic preaching its theocentric slant: "Gott behält die Initiative zu machtvollen Taten, die Herrschaft über Zeit und Geschichte des Volkes Israel und der Völker."[45] M. Weiss[46] puts it in a nutshell: "The DL (day of the Lord — W.S.P.) *per se* signifies the action of the Lord, his might- and power-potential." Thus the author of Joel takes a known tradition which he then puts to distinctive use. Whereas similar passages, such as Ez 30 2 and Isa 13 6 use the expression qarôb jôm jhwh to pronounce judgment on foreign nations, Joel 1 15 (like Am 5 18—20) applies it as a warning to his own people.[47]

In Joel 1 15, then, the Yom tradition serves to stress the imminence[48]of the Day, and its association with a crisis situation of which Yahweh himself is the "Urheber".[49]

(WMANT 27), 1968, 130 ff., also rejects Von Rad's thesis, claiming that with one solitary exception (Zeph 1) all Von Rad's texts for explaining the origin of the Yom date from exilic or postexilic times. In his view the instances Von Rad uses to explain the origin of the Yom Yahweh tradition in fact represent a later stage in its development. M. Weiss, The origin of the Day of the Lord — Reconsidered, HUCA 37 (1966), 29—60 also rejects Von Rad's thesis. He concludes that "the DL motif-complex does not hark back to an ancient 'HW tradition' but has its roots in the ancient motif-complex of the theophany-descriptions" (60). Cf. also J. Bourke, Le Jour de Yahvé dans Joël, RB 66 (1959), 5—31 and 91—212. J. Jeremias, Theophanie, Die Geschichte einer alttestamentlichen Gattung, WMANT 10, ²1977, 98 ff. points out the close relation between the Yom Yahweh tradition and the Gattung, "Theophanieschilderungen".

P. A. Verhoef, Die Dag van die Here (Exegetica 11/3), 85, maintains that the origin of all future expectations including the Yom Yahweh must be sought in the "special revelation". F. C. Fensham, A possible origin of the concept of the Day of the Lord, (Biblical Essays 1966 — Proceedings of the ninth meeting of Die Ou-Testamentiese Werkgemeenskap in Suid-Afrika), writes on the strength of parallels in Hetitite and Assyrian treaty-curses (96): ". . . the real background of this concept is a day of visitation and execution of curses." W. Vosloo, Op soek na die oorsprong van die begrip, Die dag van die Here, ThEv (Sept. 1975), 183—189, relates the Abrahamic covenant and the concomitant promises to the origin of the Yom; Y. Hoffmann, The Day of the Lord as a concept and a term in the prophetic literature, ZAW 93 (1981), 37—50, believes that the term should be studied diachronically since it underwent a metamorphosis in the course of time.

[44] E. Kutsch, Heuschreckenplage und Tag Jahwes in Joel 1 und 2, TZ 18 (1962), 89.
[45] Saebø, TWAT III/6—7, 585—586.
[46] HUCA 37 (1966), 47.
[47] Allen, op. cit., 59.
[48] A. J. Everson, The Days of Yahweh, JBL 93 (1974), 331.
[49] Kutsch, op. cit., 83.

But the pericope contains other *traditional* material as well: fire ('eš) and flame (læhabā) (19a, 19b and 20c) are standard images to proclaim judgment and destruction (cf. e. g. Am 7 4; Jer 5 14; 15 14; 17 4; Ps 50 3). Conceivably the image was chosen because flame and fire are also elements of the theophany and therefore would further accentuate the impending Yom Yahweh.[50]

The *redaction history* of the pericope calls for comment. Here the crux is 1 15 and relates to Duhm's conception of the redaction history of the book. According to Duhm[51] Joel 1 and 2 describe an ordinary locust plague. Chapters 3 and 4 were written by a second-century apocalyptic Maccabean author who also made minor additions to the first two chapters. Chapter 1 15 is alleged to have been such an apocalyptic addition. Duhm's hypothesis became the accepted view of the redaction history of Joel among literary critics and was widely influential.[52]

Our analysis of the pericope so far militates against 1 15 being such a later redactional addition. Contextually it fits in very well, and even serves an important function in the structure of 1 2—20 in that it helps to interpret the crisis as a portent of an even greater catastrophe, the Yom Yahweh.[53]

On the strength of this exegesis we may now attempt the following synthesis of the *theology* of this pericope.

Our analysis has shown that the Yom is focal. Pericope section A is more closely specified by B and C. In A the stereotyped cry of terror at once focuses attention on the Yom: this day, a day of destruction, is near. Above all it is part of Yahweh's punitive action. Hence in Joel the Yom is not a serene day of peace. The accent is on Yahweh's powerful initiative. He is the author of the crisis situation. These portents of the Yom Yahweh affect the *whole community* — cultus, economy, the lot. It is not to be averted (B).

Man and beast alike suffer under the catastrophe, resulting in a common cry of distress, a prayer to Yahweh (C). Here the summons to a collective lament (1 5—14) is intensified to an actual cry of distress.

---

[50] Rudolph, KAT XIII/2, 49.

[51] Cf. B. Duhm, Israels Propheten, ²1922 especially 398; and B. Duhm, Anmerkungen zu den Zwölf Propheten, ZAW 31 (1911), 185.

[52] Cf. e. g. Bewer, op. cit., 86; Robinson, op. cit., 61; A. Jepsen, Kleine Beiträge zum Zwölf-prophetenbuch, ZAW 15 (1938), 86; H. Birkeland, Zum hebräischen Traditionswesen. Die Komposition der prophetischen Bücher des Alten Testaments, 1938, 64; R. E. Wolfe, The Editing of the book of the Twelve, ZAW 53 (1935), 103.

[53] H. Irsigler, op. cit., 327, cf. 35, footnote 2.

Because the portents of the Yom Yahweh are described analogously to the locust plague, it becomes clear that Joel regards the locusts and all that goes with them as *portents of the Yom*. Hence the present emergency is also interpreted as an act of Yahweh, serving as a prelude to the even greater catastrophe of the Yom Yahweh. One could therefore argue that the premise is theocentric: in all these things Yahweh is at work.

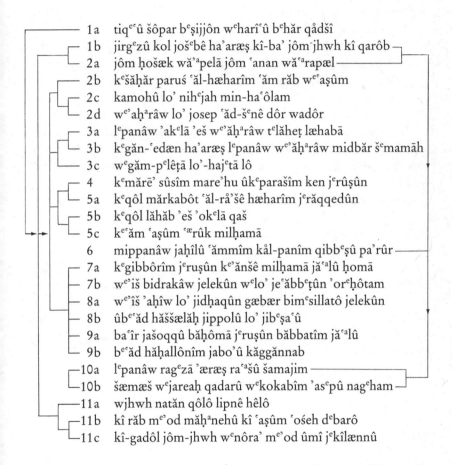

1a	tiqᵉᶜû šôpar bᵉṣijjôn wᵉharîᶜû bᵉhăr qådšî
1b	jirgᵉzû kol jošᵉbê haʾaræṣ kî-baʾ jôm‾jhwh kî qarôb
2a	jôm ḥošæk wăᵃᵃpelā jôm ᶜanan wăᵃᵃrapæl
2b	kᵉšăḥăr paruś ᶜăl-hæharîm ᶜăm răb wᵉᶜaṣûm
2c	kamohû loʾ nihᶜjah min-haᶜôlam
2d	wᵉᶜaḥᵃrâw loʾ josep ᶜăd-šᵉnê dôr wadôr
3a	lᵉpanâw ʾakᵉlā ʾeš wᵉᶜăḥᵃrâw tᵉlăheṭ læhabā
3b	kᵉgăn-ᶜedæn haʾaræṣ lᵉpanâw wᵉᶜăḥᵃrâw midbăr šᵉmamāh
3c	wᵉgăm-pᵉlêṭā loʾ-hajᵉtā lô
4	kᵉmărēʾ sûsîm mareʾhu ûkᵉparašîm ken jᵉrûṣûn
5a	kᵉqôl mărkabôt ᶜăl-râʾšê hæharîm jᵉrăqqedûn
5b	kᵉqôl lăhăb ʾeš ʾokᵉlā qaš
5c	kᵉᶜăm ᶜaṣûm ᶜærûk milḥamā
6	mippanâw jaḥîlû ᶜămmîm kål-panîm qibbᵉṣû paʾrûr
7a	kᵉgibbôrîm jᵉruṣûn kᵉʾănšê milḥamā jăᶜᵃlû ḥomā
7b	wᵉʾiš bidrakâw jelekûn wᵉloʾ jeᶜăbbᵉṭûn ʾorᵉḥôtam
8a	wᵉʾiš ʾaḥîw loʾ jidḥaqûn gæbær bimᵉsillatô jelekûn
8b	ûbᵉᶜăd hăššælăḥ jippolû loʾ jibᵉṣaᶜû
9a	baᶜîr jašoqqû băḥômā jᵉruṣûn băbbatîm jăᶜᵃlû
9b	bᵉᶜăd hăḥallônîm jaboʾû kăggănnab
10a	lᵉpanâw ragᵉzā ʾæræṣ raᶜᵃšû šamajim
10b	šæmæš wᵉjareaḥ qadarû wᵉkokabîm ʾasᵉpû nagᵉham
11a	wjhwh natăn qôlô lipnê hêlô
11b	kî răb mᵉᶜod măḥᵃnehû kî ᶜaṣûm ᶜośeh dᵉbarô
11c	kî-gadôl jôm-jhwh wᵉnôraʾ mᵉᶜod ûmî jᵉkîlænnû

This pericope presents plenty of exegetical problems, the chief one being whether it is a description of an actual locust plague or an apocalyptic army.

As far as demarcation is concerned, however, there is a fair measure of agreement. Chapter 2 1 opens with a stereotyped introductory formula (ti-qᵉᶜu šôpar). The pericope moreover reveals a certain completeness in that it starts and finishes with the theme of the Yom Yahweh. The *content*, too, is unified with its description of the army, and its *Gattung* sets it apart from both the preceding pericope (1 15–20) and the succeeding 2 12–17. In addition 2 1 contains a conspicuous "new" *tradition* (Zion). The *Stichwort*, panîm/panâw (cf. 3a, 3b, 6 (× 2), 10a, 11a) occurs repeatedly. C. A. Keller writes:[1] "Cette analyse prouve que la péricope est unité littéraire, un poème complet et cohérent ..."

Nonetheless the repetition of words serves to forge close links with the preceding pericopes. The Yom Yahweh of 1 15b features again (cf. 2 2a/b; 2 11c). 2 1b with its jirgᵉzû kol jošᵉbê haʾaræṣ strikingly resembles hăʾᵃzînû kol jošᵉbê haʾaræṣ (1 2a); both expressions occur at the beginning of their respective pericopes. Equally manifest are the resemblances between 1 6a (ʿaṣûm wᵉʿên mispar) and 2 2b (ʿăm răb wᵉʿaṣûm), and 1 3b (lᵉdôr ʾăḥer) and 2 2d (ʿăd-šᵉnê dôr wadôr). 2 3a is an almost verbatim repetition of 1 19b and 1 20c. The author is clearly forging a deliberate link between this pericope and the ones preceding it. Thus 2 1–11 is not an altogether new departure. It would be more true to say that it represents yet another *Steigerung* on the preceding pericopes.

Although the *text-critical* problems are not very serious, they warrant mentioning. The first one occurs in 2 2b, involving merely a change in vocalization. It has been suggested that šăḥăr ("the red glow of dawn") should be changed to šᵉḥor ("darkness", "gloom").[2] As a rule it is argued that in view of 2a, with its accent on the darkness of the Yom Yahweh, šᵉḥor would be the best reading here as well. There is no decisive evidence, however, to change the Massoretic vocalization.[3] The *tertium comparationis* lies in indicating the sudden arrival and magnitude of the "army". The other "text-critical" problems in this pericope are actually *semantic* (*hapax legomena*), but there is no weighty evidence to emendate the text.[4]

---

[1] Keller, op. cit., 123.

[2] Cf. Thompson, IB 6, 143; Bewer, op. cit., 95–96; Robinson, op. cit., 60; Allen, op. cit., 68–69; Sellin, op. cit., 157; cf. also BHS *ad loc.*

[3] Kutsch, op. cit., 83; Deden op. cit., 97. M. Bič, op. cit., 49–50; Rudolph, KAT XIII/2, 51; Weiser, ATD, 114; Wolff, BKAT XIV/2, 52; Kapelrud retains the vocalization šăḥăr but attaches mythological significance to it, cf. op. cit., 73–74. Cf. also Keller, op. cit., 125 footnote 2.

[4] Cf. BHK[3] and BHS for the various problems. The following problems may also be noted: 6: paʾrûr (probably "glow" or "heat" – cf. also Nah 2 11, the only other incidence) is sometimes changed to parûr ("cooking pot"). There is however no reason for this (cf. commentaries ad loc.). The meaning of hăššælaḥ (8b) also poses problems. Most translators and commentaries render it with "weapons". W. Rudolph, SVT 16 (1965), 248 and Rudolph, KAT XIII/2, 51 relate it to the tunnel of Shiloam in the reign of Hezekiah. (For the various other proposals see the above two works by Rudolph). Rudolph's idea could be over-sub-

The *formal structure* of the pericope may be described as follows: there is a close link between *1b*, with its summons to the kol još^ebê ha'aræṣ, substantiated by the imminence of the Yom Yahweh, and *2a* where the Yom is described in more detail by means of four adjectives (ḥošæk, ʾᵃpela, ʿanan, ʿᵃrapæl). The obvious aim is to stress the darkness. The effect of the synonymous parallelism in 2a is also emphatic. Theoretically baʾ in 1b could be either a perfect or a participle, but in view of the closer qualification kî qarôb it must be seen as a participle.⁵ The day is at hand, is impending, but has not yet come. Yet there is indisputably a progression between 1 15 (kî qarôb jôm jhwh ... jabôʾ) and 2 1b (ki·baʾ jôm·jhwh kî qarôb). Here the Yom Yahweh is depicted as even closer at hand.

2 2b introduces a new subject (ʿăm). There is a close link between 2b and 2c due to the conspicuous position of the particle kᵉ in both; in 2c there is a reiteration of ʿăm via a third person masculine pronominal suffix, kamohû. The syntactic connection between 2c and 2d is strengthened further by the recurrence of the third person suffix in 2d (ʾaḥᵃrâw), and by the striking waw copulative in 2d. The loʾ plus verb in both stichs, as well as the temporal expressions min-haʿôlam (2c) and ʿăd-šᵉnê dôr wadôr (2d), further underscore the connection between them. Thus 2c and 2d are a more detailed description of the ʿăm răb ʿaṣûm. These stichs, 2b, c and d, stress the peerless uniqueness of this mighty army, thus representing the convergence and climax of the descriptions of the extraordinary event (săpperû ... lᵉdôr ʾᵃher − 1 3ab) and the mighty nation (ʿaṣûm wᵉʾên mispar − 1 6a).

2 3aff. continues to describe the army. This is evident from the repetition of the third person suffixes (lᵉpanâw, ʾăḥᵃrâw-3a; lᵉpanâw, ʾăḥᵃrâw-3b). The two hemistichs of 3a are parallels, and 3b is structured chiastically:

kᵉgăn·ʿedæn ... lᵉpanâw // ʾăḥᵃrâw ... šᵉmamāh
   a   b   b   a

3a and 3b both deal with the dramatic contrast between conditions prior to the advent of the army (lᵉpanâw) and those after it had marched

---

jectively linked to his dating of the book. The connotation "weapons" fits into the context. The *hapax legomenon* jᵉʿăbbᵉṭûn need not automatically change the text. The meaning of the verb emerges fairly clearly from the context ("deviate from course"). C. F. Whitley, ʿbṭ in Joel 2, 7, Biblica 65 (1984), 101–102, regards ʿbṭ as a variant of ḥbṭ (decline, turn aside from).

⁵ Cf. Allen, op. cit., 64; Wolff, BKAT XIV/2, 51; Kapelrud, op. cit., 71; Bewer, op. cit., 101; Bič, op. cit., 49; Rudolph, KAT XIII/2, 51; contra H. G. Reventlow, Prophetisches Ich bei Jeremia, 1963, 115 ("Was in Wirklichkeit noch Zukunft ist, ist in der Schau des Propheten bereits vollendete Gegenwart"). Cf. also Keller, op. cit., 120.

past (ˀăḥᵃrâw.) This army radically changed the prevailing order. The emphatic wᵉgăm in 3c is overarchingly linked with 3a/b and stresses the impossibility of escaping from the army.

Another important point is that the catastrophe depicted in the preceding pericope section (1 15–20) – kîˀeš ˀakᵉlā (19), læhabā lihᵃṭa (19c), see also 20c – is here described analogously as the havoc wrought by the "army". The uniqueness of this army (loˀ nihᵉjah – 2c; loˀ jôsep – 2d) is analogously described as its inescapability (wᵉgăm⁻pᵉlêṭā loˀ⁻hajᵉtā lô).

4–5c constitute a new pericope section marked by military terminology (parašîm, sûsim – 4; mărkabôt – 5a; ᶜᵃrûk milḥamā – 5c). The kᵉ, repeated four times, is equally conspicuous. Verses 4 and 5a would appear to be linked even more closely: the metre is long; the two stichs rhyme (jᵉrûṣûn, jᵉrăqqᵉdûn); both contain third person plural verbs. 5b and 5c are similarly linked: both are written in strikingly short metre, both contain nominal sentences and participles. These two pairs of stichs (4/5a, 5b/c) are ingeniously joined together by the marked repetition of kᵉqôl in 5a and 5b. The pericope uses four (kᵉ × 4) images to describe the army. The soldiers look and run like horses (4); they make a noise like chariots leaping across mountain tops(!) (5a); the noise is like that of burning stubble (5b); and they are like a mighty army arranged for battle. The *Stichwort* ᶜăm ᶜaṣûm from 2 2b is reiterated and elaborated to ᶜăm ᶜaṣûm ᶜᵃrûk milḥamā. The ˀăl-hæharîm from 2b is also repeated in 5a: ˀăl-răˀšê hæharîm. In 2 5b the army (kᵉqôl lăhăb ˀeš ˀokᵉlā qaš) is once again described analogously to the catastrophe of the earlier pericopes (cf. 1 19b, 19c, 20c; 1 6a). Thus it would appear to be a repeat of the same disaster (locusts accompanied by drought), but now it is expressed more dramatically and urgently to stress the imminence of the Yom Yahweh. To this end the poet exercises his poetic licence and uses hyperboles to describe the army. The imperfects in this and the ensuing verses have the archaic -ûn ending (jᵉrûṣûn-4; jᵉrăqqedûn-5a; jᵉruṣ-ûn-7a; jelekûn-7b; jᵉᶜăbbetûn-7b; jidḥaqûn, jelekûn-8a; jᵉruṣûn-9a). These "are used purposely to bring out the whole weight and power of the attack, they deepen the impression of terror and awe".[6] The effect is enhanced by the reiteration of jᵉrûṣûn, (4; 7a; 9a) and other verbs expressing movement and velocity (cf. e.g. jelekûn-7b, 8a).

2 6 fits quite neatly into the whole: the *Stichwort* panîm recurs twice in this stich, and the high frequency third person suffix, mippanâw, is reiterated. Yet in this stich we have a manifestly new subject – ᶜammîm. From the

---

[6] Bewer, op. cit., 98; Rudolph, KAT XIII/2, 56; Wolff, BKAT XIV/2, 53; Allen, op. cit., 71.

context it is perfectly clear that the mippanâw can only refer to the army (locusts!)[7]. The description of this mighty army is resumed in 2 7, so that 2 6 is a more or less parenthetic account of the reaction of the ʾămmîm to the ʿăm ʿaṣûm. There appears to be some sort of intensification of this reaction: in 2 1b it was a *national* response — kol jošᵉbê haʾăræṣ clearly refers to Judah, see also 1 2a; in 2 6 it has expanded into an *international* reaction, ʿămmim.

2 7–9 is another pericope section, the same subject featuring throughout. This is evident particularly from the third person plural imperfects (jᵉruṣûn, jăʿᵃlû-7a; jelekûn, jeʿăbbᵉṭûn-7b; jidḥaqûn, jelekûn-8a, jippolû, jibᵉṣaʿû-8b; jašoqqû, jᵉruṣun, jăʿᵃlû-9a; jaboʾû-9b).

At 2 10 the subject changes once more. Basically the various stichs of 2 7–9 are all interlinked at the same level, yet one should note the different devices the poet uses to describe the violence of the "army's" onslaught. 2 7a contains a parallelism, 7b a chiasmus:

weʾîš bidrakâw jelekûn   //   weʾloʾ jeʿăbbᵉṭûn ʾorᵉḥôtam
   a   b   b   a

Between 7b and 8a there are indications of a further chiasmus as regards the particle loʾ and the verbs:
7b jelekûn + loʾ
8a loʾ   + jelekûn

Note that both 7b and 8a are introduced by the prominently positioned weʾiš, and that both stichs contain the third person singular pronominal suffix (bidrakâw-7b; ʾaḥîw-8a). A striking feature of 8b, 9a and 9b is that all three these stichs start with the preposition bᵉ, and 8b and 9b moreover start with the corresponding bᵉʿăd. Several lexeme repetitions occur in this pericope section: jᵉruṣûn 7a and 9a; jăʿᵃlû 7a and 9a; jelekûn 7b and 8a; gibbôrîm and gæbær 7a and 8a; ḥomā 7a and 9a. One observes that no fewer than three words from 7a recur in 9a, while the *Stichwort*, milḥamā, from 5c in the preceding section is also repeated (7a). The language and terminology indicate that this pericope describes the attack of the army and capture of the city. By means of lexeme repetitions and the various stylistic and syntactic devices we have mentioned the poet manages to describe these events in a much accentuated, dramatic way.

At 10a, we said, the subject changes once more: ʾæræṣ, šamajim, šæmæš, jareaḥ, kokabîm are the subjects of 10a and 10b, which are natural-

---

[7] Cf. Rudolph, KAT XIII/2, 56.

ly interlinked. There is some disagreement among scholars as to whom is
referred to by the third person singular suffix lᵉpanâw in 10a. E. Kutsch[8]
feels that it refers to Yahweh, arguing that there is a close connection between 10b and 11a because of the subject-predicate sequence in both and
the copulative. In addition he sees the three kî sentences as causal clauses.
He claims that 10a continues logically and syntactically in 11a and 11b, and
on the strength of this he concludes that lᵉpanâw also refers to Yahweh. W.
Rudolph[9] proved convincingly that this suffix cannot but refer to the
"army." In addition Kutsch's argument that there is no syntactic or sub-
stantial connection between 10a and 10b does not hold water. In terms of
content the two stichs are closely related in that both concern a *cosmic* reaction. The adverbial lᵉpanâw in 10a applies to 10b as well. The verb-subject
sequence of 10a, which in 10b is inverted to subject-verb, cannot be used to
prove a syntactic division. Earlier in the same poem (see 7b and 8a) the poet
used this very same stylistic device to effect a chiasmus. If one refuses to
regard the kî clauses in 11b and 11c as motivative clauses (see discussion
below) the problem is solved. After all, Kutsch[10] himself showed that the
passage is meaningless if one regards these clauses as the direct substantiation for 11a. The lᵉpanâw refers to the ʿăm ʿaṣum, and hence 10a and 10b
describe a cosmic reaction, enhanced by the climactic structure of the pericope. First we have a local, *national* reaction in 2 1b; this is followed by an
international (2 6), and finally by a *cosmic* reaction (2 10ab) to the ʿăm
ʿasûm. It is remarkable that the same verb used to describe Judah's reaction
in 2 1b (rgz) should be used again in 2 10b to describe the cosmic reaction.
Not until 11a is Yahweh explicitly named as commander of this army.

   At 11a the subject changes dramatically: for the first time in the book
Yahweh is directly shown to be the subject. The waw should most likely be
seen as an explicative waw. 2 11a, b and c are strung together simply by
means of stichs starting with kî. These three consecutive kî clauses in 11a
and 11c cannot possibly be causal: surely it would be illogical to cite the
magnitude of Yahweh's army (11b/c) to substantiate the fact that he leads
his army. The only logical solution is to interpret the kî as an affirmative
kî.[11] The three successive kî clauses and the rhetorical question (ûmî jᵉ-
kîlænnû), presupposing a negative answer, all stress the greatness and terri-
fying nature of the Day of the Lord.

---

[8] TZ 18 (1962), 88; cf. also Wolff, BKAT XIV/2, 56.
[9] Cf. KAT XIII/2, ad loc.
[10] Op. cit., 87.
[11] Cf. Keller, op. cit., 123.

The *metre* of this poem consists predominantly of *Doppeldreiers*.[12] Bewer writes as follows about the 2 + 2 metre in 9:[13] "The staccato character of the rhythm is evidently intended, it brings out the movement of the advancing and attacking hosts with great realism. The rhythmic tone corresponds exactly to the graphic description and heightens its effect." The different pericope sections are interrelated as follows: 2b–2d, 3a–3c, 4–5 and 7a–9b are interlinked since all of them have the same subject – the ʿăm ʿaṣûm. The action of the ʿăm ʿaṣûm is described climactically. Verses 1b–2a, 6 and 10a/b are connected since they deal with the reaction to the ʿăm ʿaṣûm and the Yom Yahweh.[14] This reaction too is described climactically. First it is only Judah (2 1b), then the ʿammîm (2 6), and then the reaction becomes a cosmic one. This section on the reaction manifests an *inclusio* in that it starts and ends with the verb rgz (2 1b and 2 10a).

Verse 11a, b and c – the climax of the pericope – links up with the preceding 1b–10b. The hêlô refers to the ʿăm ʿaṣûm, elaborately explained in the preceding section. Yahweh is mentioned as the commander of the army. The passage 1b–11c manifests another *inclusio*, beginning and ending with the Yom Yahweh, which thus constitutes a framework for the pericope as a whole and also reflects its central theme. Hence the overarching summons in 1a (tiqᵉʿû ... harîʿû) relates directly to the Yom Yahweh.

The *Gattung* of the pericope is best described as an *Alarmbefehl mit Feindschilderung*.[15] H.-P. Müller[16] maintains that it is an even greater summons to a national lament emanating from 1 5–14. In his view the parallels between this passage and 2 15 clinch the argument. But Müller's view does not stand up to scrutiny: thus 2 1–11 does not have the same formal attributes as 1 5–14 (see discussion above) to qualify as another summons to a national lament.

Wolff[17] is right in claiming that the remarkable feature of this *Alarmbefehl* is that it is used to proclaim the impending Yom and to accentuate its ominous nature. This *Gattung* is also marked by theophanic descriptions (see particulars below), indicating Yahweh as the real commander of this

---

[12] Cf. Sellin, op. cit., 158; T. H. Robinson, op. cit., 61; Allen, op. cit., 64–66; Wolff, BKAT XIV/2, 47; Kapelrud, op. cit., 124 observes that 2 1–11 is a rare instance of a "somewhat regular rhythm" in Joel.

[13] Op. cit., 100.

[14] Kutsch, op. cit., 87 rightly points out that the two stichs converge at this point.

[15] Wolff, BKAT XIV/2, 45–46; H.-M. Lütz, op. cit., 34; M. Bič, op. cit., 48, talks about an "Aufruf zur Bereitschaft".

[16] Theologia Viatorum 10 (1965/6), 235–236.

[17] Wolff, BKAT XIV/2, 45.

hostile force. The first person singular suffix (bᵉḥăr qådšî) in 2 1a tells us that the speaker is Yahweh himself. He personally issues the *Alarmbefehl*. Another point to be noted is that the pericope has some of the stylistic features of descriptions of apocalyptic visions.[18]

As for *traditions* and other stereotyped matter, 2 1–11 has much to offer. In 2 1a the *Zion tradition* emerges, associated not with salvation and security but with the *Alarmbefehl*, the ominously impending *Yom Yahweh*. This latter tradition is also used here to proclaim a day of doom rather than salvation. The Yom Yahweh tradition is described in conventional terms. The terms ḥošæk wăᵃpelā (2 2a) occur in several Old Testament passages,[19] and in Am 5 20 and Zeph 1 15 they are also used with reference to the Yom Yahweh. Interestingly the locust plague in Ex 10 22 is described in similar terms. In 2 2a we find a second conventional formula, ʿanan wăᵃ-ræpæl.[20] In Zeph 1 15 it is also used in connection with the Yom Yahweh. This formula is used both in Dtn 4 11 and Ps 97 2 to describe the theophany. Thus we find that 2 2a uses conventional theophanic terminology to describe the Yom. Very important too is the fact that the depiction of the theophany in 2 2a (ʿanan wăᵃrapæl) relates closely to the *Sinai-Horeb* traditions.[21] One could argue that the God of Sinai is here depicted as the commander of an invincible army.[22]

Ps 97 3 contains another parallel, this time for 2 3a. Of course the fire preceding Yahweh in Ps 97 3 relates to the theophany as well. pᵉlêṭa (2 3c) is another instance of military terminology.[23]

In 2 3b the garden of Eden *motif*, normally used as a symbol of fertility and plenty,[24] indicates the contrast between conditions before and after the coming of the army. This motif is used in similar fashion in Isa 51 3 and Ez 36 35.

Jorg Jeremias[25] points out the likelihood that the two motifs — that of the voice of Yahweh[26] and of the earthquake[27] — of the Yom Yahweh tradition in 2 10–11 were probably derived from the theophany accounts. In Isa

---

[18] Cf. this pericope with Ez 1 26–28; 8 2; 10 1; 40 3; 42 11; 43 3.
[19] Cf. e.g. Ex 10 22; Am 5 20; Zeph 1 15; Isa 58 10 and 59 9.
[20] Cf. e.g. Dtn 4 11; Ps 97 2; Zeph 1 15; Ez 34 12.
[21] Cf. H. Irsigler, Gottesgericht und Jahwetag, 1977, 357ff.
[22] Wolff, op. cit., 62.
[23] Cf. Jdc 21 17; II Sam 15 14.
[24] Cf. e. g. Gen 2 8ff.; 13 10; Ez 28 13; 31 9, 16, 18.
[25] Theophanie, 1977, 99.
[26] Cf. e.g. Ex 19 16ff.; Ps 29.
[27] Cf. e.g. Jdc 5 4; Ps 18 8; 68 9; 77 19.

13 13 and Ez 38 19−20 they also occur in conjunction with the Yom Yahweh. The darkening of the sun, moon and stars as a sign of the Yom Yahweh also occurs in Isa 13 10. Joel 2 1−11 has many parallels with Isa 13 − it
may even be dependant on it[28] − yet the author of Joel uses his material in a
highly individual way. Thus Isa 13 is a poem pronouncing judgment on
Babylon, whereas in Joel 2 1−11 Yahweh is addressing Jerusalem.

The conventional formula gadôl, nôra' in 2 11c describing the Yom
Yahweh occurs elsewhere in the Old Testament to describe the great and
awesome nature of Yahweh's deeds.[29]

From all this it is clear that this pericope contains a great deal of conventional material, mainly from the theophany account associated with the
Yom Yahweh tradition.

One's conception of the *redaction history* of 2 1−11 will once again
depend on how one sees the redaction history of the book as a whole. Usually it is contended that 2 1b−2a and 2 10−11 were added by a "Day of
Yahweh Editor" or an "Apokalyptiker"[30] but our exegesis has shown that
these passages are structurally and as regards content so much part of the
pericope that they could not possibly have been later additions.

On the basis of the foregoing exegesis one could trace the following
theological trends. The circular structure of the pericope focuses attention
on the Yom Yahweh. This day is once again depicted as dark, ominous and
fearsome.

By contrast with the preceding − a cry of distress to Yahweh − this
one is an *Alarmbefehl* issued by Yahweh: all the inhabitants of Judah must
tremble for the dark, inescapable Day of Yahweh is at hand. The Lord's
anger is turned first of all on his own people. Kutsch[31] summarizes it aptly:
"In den Heuschrecken wird also Gottes Gerichts- und Strafwillen transpar-
ent."

The description of the catastrophe associated with the Yom Yahweh is
analogous to those in previous pericopes. Hence this is not a matter of a
fresh disaster, nor of whether it is a real locust plague or an apocalyptic
army. It is rather an intensified version of one and the same event (locust

---

[28] For a discussion of the relation between Joel 2 1−11 and Isa 13, cf. Wolff, BKAT XIV/2,
    55−56. Kutsch, op. cit., 92.
[29] Cf. e.g. Dtn 7 21; 20 21; Ps 106 21ff.
[30] Cf. e.g. B. Duhm, Israels Propheten, 398; R. E. Wolfe, The Editing of the book of the
    Twelve, ZAW 53 (1935), 90−129; Sellin, op. cit., 158; A. Jepsen, ZAW 56 (1938), 86−87;
    Bewer, op. cit., 94−95, 103.
[31] Heuschreckenplage und Tag Jahwes in Joel 1 und 2, TZ 18 (1962), 94.

plague *cum* drought), here used to describe the imminent Day of the Lord. The account of the "army's" attack on and capture of the city is dramatic to the point of hyperbole: the army is like no other army (2 2b–c), it brings devastation and radical change to the existing order, and none can escape it (2 3a, b and c).

The crucial point of the entire pericope, however, is that Yahweh personally commands this army. He himself speaks (2 1), hence the army is executing his orders (2 11). This means that Yahweh personally controls the "portents" of his Day. But the description of the army combines elements of a theophany account, from which one infers that it actually refers to the coming of Yahweh. One realizes that behind the onslaught of the locust-like army Yahweh himself is at work.[32]

The Yom is a day of judgment evoking a divine *Alarmbefehl* from Zion against Judah, but it has international and cosmic repercussions as well. The function of the *Zion tradition* is therefore not the usual one of proclaiming salvation, but to sound an alarm. Nor is the significance of the day ephemeral and localized: its impact is universal.

The function of this pericope is to warn the Lord's people because –
+ the great and terrible Day of the Lord is near – a day not of salvation, but of doom and disaster; and
+ Yahweh personally commands the army associated with this day, hence the people are faced with the awesome arrival of the Lord himself.

This pericope is fully integrated with the preceding ones, but at the same time reflects a *Steigerung*[33] in that the Day of the Lord is depicted as even more imminent and ominous. What is more, Yahweh himself is behind these events.

---

[32] H.-M. Lutz, Jahwe, Jerusalem und die Völker, 1968, 37.
[33] Cf. Wolff, BKAT XIV/2, 48 and earlier pages where this matter is expounded in detail.

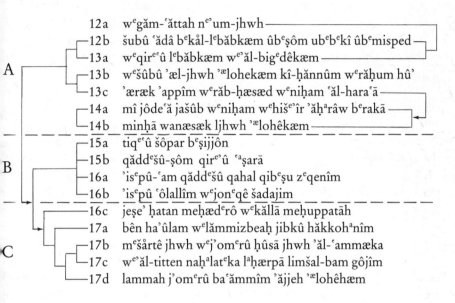

12a wᵉgăm-ᶜăttah nᵉᵓum-jhwh
12b šubû ᶜădâ bᵉkăl-lᵉbăbkæm ûbᵉṣôm ubᵉbᵉkî ûbᵉmisped
13a wᵉqirᵉᶜû lᵉbăbkæm wᵉᵓăl-bigᵉdêkæm
A
13b wᵉšûbû ᵓæl-jhwh ᵓælohekæm kî-ḥănnûm wᵉrăḥum hûᵓ
13c ᵓæræk ᵓappîm wᵉrăb-ḥæsæd wᵉniḥam ᶜăl-haraᶜā
14a mî jôdeᶜă jašûb wᵉniḥam wᵉhišᵉᵓîr ᵓăḥᵃrâw bᵉrakā
14b minḥā wanæsæk ljhwh ᵓælohêkæm

B
15a tiqᵉᶜû šôpar bᵉṣijjôn
15b qăddᵉšû-ṣôm qirᵉᵓû ᶜăṣarā
16a ᵓisᵉpû-ᶜam qăddᵉšû qahal qibᵉṣu zᵉqenîm
16b ᵓisᵉpû ᶜôlallîm wᵉjonᵉqê šadajim

C
16c ješeᵓ ḥatan meḥædᵉrô wᵉkăllā meḥuppatāh
17a bên haᵓûlam wᵉlămmizbeaḥ jibkû hăkkohᵃnîm
17b mᵉšårtê jhwh wᵉjᵓomᵉrû ḥûsā jhwh ᵓăl-ᶜammæka
17c wᵉᵓăl-titten naḥᵃlatᵉka lᵃḥærpā limšal-bam gôjîm
17d lammah jᵓomᵉrû baᶜămmîm ᵓăjjeh ᵓælohêhæm

The waw copulative before găm should be regarded as an *adversative* particle.[1] According to Wolff, wᵉgăm has an "additiv-steigernde"[2] function. Kapelrud[3] rightly points out that the wᵉgăm ᶜăttah ". . . serves to emphasize that the hour is late and Yahweh's Day nigh at hand, but even now there is a respite, even now there may be hope if Yahweh is appealed to".

At 2 18 there is a marked *change of subject*. The unity of the pericope also resides in its pronounced focus on the cultus, evident mainly from the terminology used: ṣôm, bᵉkî, misped-12b; bᵉrakā-14a; minḥā wanæsæk-14b; qăddᵉšû-ṣôm, qirᵉᵓû ᶜăṣarā-15b; qăddᵉšû qahal-16a; ᵓûlam, mizbeaḥ, kohᵃnim-17a. Formally 2 12–17 is also characterized by a string of *imperatives* (šubû-12b; qirᵉᵓû-13a; šûbû-13b; tiqᵉᶜû-15a; qăddᵉšû, qirᵉᵓû-15b; ᵓisᵉ-

---

[1] Cf. E. Sellin, op. cit., 161.
[2] Wolff, BKAT XIV/2, 57.
[3] Op. cit., 81.

pû, qădd^ešû, qib^eṣu-16a; ʾis^epû-16b) and, from 16c onwards, by jussives
(jeṣeʾ-16c; jibkû-17a; jʾom^erû-17b).

There are not noteworthy *text-critical problems* attached to this pericope.

As for its *structure*, the following: 12b and 13a are linked for various
reasons. These two stichs form part of the *Gottesrede* where Yahweh speaks
in the first person. From 13b onwards Yahweh is again the topic of discussion. The l^ebăbkæm of 12b is repeated in 13a. A striking feature of 12b is
the preposition b^e repeated four times in succession: b^ekål, b^eṣôm, b^eb^ekî,
b^emisped. This is probably intended to underscore the seriousness of the
appeal.

13b and c are linked. 13c continues, by means of nominal clauses the
description of Yahweh's "attributes" in 13b. 14a and b are linked in that
14b, lacking a verb, depends syntactically on 14a. Both stichs describe
"possible" courses of action by Yahweh. In 14a there is a striking pun,
when the word šub, used to summon the people to penitence (cf. 2 12b;
13b) is used to describe Yahweh's possible "repentance". This forges a
close link between the penitence of the people and Yahweh's response to
it.[4]

Stich 12a is linked with 12b/13a since the latter two lines clearly render
the substance of the *Gottesrede* (n^{eʾ}um-jhwh) in 12a. Lines 13b/c form a
link between the preceding 12a/b/c and the ensuing 14a/b. Lines 13b/c are
on the one hand linked with 12b/13a: the imperatives continue and the waw
copulative indicates a connection. By contrast with the šubû ʿădâ in 12b we
have w^ešûbû ʾæl-jhwh. But 13b/c also links up with 14a/b: niḥam which is
found in 13c occurs again in 14a; like 13c, 14a/b describes Yahweh's action.

15a to 16b are all linked at the same level on account of the chain of
imperatives[5] (tiq^{eʾ}û-15a; qădd^ešû-15b; ʾis^epû-16a; ʾis^epû-16c). In 16a a lexeme (qădd^ešû) from 15b is repeated, and one from 16a (ʾis^epû) recurs in 16b.
Probably these repetitions are meant to heighten the urgency of the sum-
mons. Note that 2 15 is virtually a verbatim repetition of 2 1 (tiq^{eʾ}û šôpar),
and 2 15b of 1 14 (qadd^ešû-ṣôm qir^{eʾ}û ʿaṣarā.) When viewing the macro-
structure one would have to inquire into the function of these repetitions
and establish whether their meaning remains the same in each new context.

---

[4] M. Bič, op. cit., 60.

[5] Bewer, op. cit., 107, regards 2 15–17 as a unit and vocalizes the verbs from v. 15 onwards
   as perfects rather than as imperatives. He therefore regards 15–17 as a narrative. For a
   sound refutation of Bewer's argument see Wolff, BKAT XIV/2, 67.

By contrast with the preceding section (15a–16b), the lines from 16c onwards contain jussives.[6] 17b/c/d constitutes a unit since it is direct speech following the j'om°rû in 17b. Within this unit, however, 17b and 17c are particularly closely linked: the waw copulative establishes a very obvious connection, and ḥûsā (17b) is moreover the positive imperative and 'ăl titten (17c) the negative, both addressed to Yahweh. Line 17d, introduced by the interrogative particle lammah, logically links up with the preceding line. Line 17a relates closely to the combined 17b/c/d since 17a and 17b both contain third person plural jussives (jibkû-17a; j'om°rû-17b). In addition they share the same subject (hăkkoh°nim and m°šårtê jhwh). The entire combination 17abcd is logically connected with the preceding jussive singular.

The various commentaries present a rather confusing picture of the *metre*.[7] Keller[8] rightly describes it as "irrégulier et agité". The metre in this pericope, as in most of the book of Joel, is highly irregular. One could however argue that the staccato style of 2 15–16 greatly emphasizes the urgency of the appeals.[9]

From this discussion it is evident that pericope 2 12–17 consists of three sections: 2 12–14 (A); 2 15–16b (B); and 2 16c–17 (C). B and C are connected since B (the injunction to cultic actions arising from the summons to repentance in A) is continued in C through the jussives. A links up logically with the combination BC.

The relation of this pericope to the earlier ones should also be noted. As pointed out, 2 12a has an adversative, but also an intensifying function in relation to the preceding passage: by contrast with the *Alarmbefehl* in 2 1–11, lines 2 12ff. reiterate the imminence of the Yom Yahweh, but at the same time stress that there is still hope that the people will repent. Line 2 14b strikingly resembles 1 9a and 1 13c in its use of words (minḥa wanæsæk). Whereas 1 9a and 13c concern the disruption of sacrificial worship, the latter pericope raises hopes that Yahweh will restore cultic life. Lines 2 15b and 16a are almost identical with 1 14ff., reiterating and expanding on the terminology of the latter. In a sense 2 15b–16a have their counterpart in 1 14ff., yet there is a marked progression between the two

---

[6] Keller, op. cit., 130 footnote 6 believes that jese' (16c) jibkû (17a) j'om° rû (17b and c) should be seen as "impératifs de la troisième personne" – third person imperatives.

[7] Cf. e.g. Allen, op. cit., 76–77; Sellin, op. cit., 161; T. H. Robinson, op. cit., 63; Bewer, op. cit., 105.

[8] Op. cit., 130.

[9] Cf. Allen, op. cit., 82; Bewer, op. cit., 108.

pericopes.[10] In the earlier pericope these verses function mainly within the context of the summons to lament, but in the later pericope there has been a development in that the terminology functions as practical cultic injunctions to people who have heeded the call to repentance (2 12—14).

2 15a (tiq$^{e^{c}}$û šôpar b^{e}ṣijjon) is a repetition of 2 1a, but again there is a *Steigerung* if one compares the two stichs with due regard to their respective contexts. In 2 1 the expression is an *Alarmbefehl* urging the people to flee from Yahweh, the commander of the army; in 2 15a it summons the people to come to Yahweh.[11] In 2 1 it is an alarm, in 2 15a a summons to a cultic gathering.[12] H. Frey[13] aptly says that 2 15 is a summons, not to take up arms, but to repent. The author's delicate play with words and the marked repetitions in the text so far lead us to suspect that the 'aḥ^{a}râw in 2 14a is not just coincidence but a deliberate reiteration of 'aḥ^{a}raw in 2 3a. Again there is a dramatic contrast: in 2 3a 'aḥ^{a}râw describes the destructive, devastating behaviour of an army led by Yahweh; in 2 14a it appears in the context of Yahweh's forgiving act of blessing.[14] Clearly, then, despite the similarities in terminology and language, there has been some development between the pericope in chapter 1 and the present one. We shall return to this point in our recapitulatory comments on the theology of the book as a whole.

For a proper grasp of the pericope one must consider the *Gattung*. Possibly one would have to differentiate between the various pericope sections. Scholars have classified the *Gattung* as follows: J. Scharbert[15] sees 2 12—14 as an appeal to the nation to repent and A. Weiser,[16] T. H. Robinson,[17] M. Bič,[18] W. Rudolph[19] and Sellin[20] describe the *Gattung* in much the same terms. L. C. Allen[21] regards it as a "national repentance" and J. A.

---

[10] For further details, see the discussion comparing the *Gattung* of 1 5—14 with that of 1 15—17.

[11] Wolff, BKAT XIV/2, 60.

[12] Deden, op. cit., 100.

[13] H. Frey, Die kleinen nachexilischen Propheten (BAT), 1948, 217.

[14] Cf. Wolff, BKAT XIV/2, 59—60.

[15] Formgeschichte und Exegese von Ex 34, 6 f. und seiner Parallelen, Biblica 38 (1957), 133.

[16] Op. cit., 114.

[17] Op. cit., 63.

[18] Op. cit., 58.

[19] Op. cit., 58.

[20] Op. cit., 161; cf. also A. Jepsen, Kleine Beiträge zum Zwölfprophetenbuch, ZAW 56 (1938), 89.

[21] Op. cit., 77.

Thompson[22] largely agrees, designating it a "call to national repentance". Deden[23] regards 2 12—17 as one entity as far as *Gattung* is concerned and calls it a liturgy for repentance. Sellin[24] points out that the mî jôde'ǎ in 14a is a stereotyped term from the liturgy of repentance (cf. Jon 3 9a). H. W. Wolff[25] defines it as a call to repentance and points out[26] that this definition is based mainly on two features of the summons to a national lament (see 1 5—14): unlike the lament, the penitence does not stem from a crisis situation (see 1 5—14), but from the acts and the will of Yahweh (see 1 13—14). Elsewhere[27] Wolff describes 2 12—14 as a prophetic admonition, pointing out that, unlike 1 5—14 (national lament) it does not merely summon the people to ritual, but to a total return to Yahweh.

H.-P. Müller[28] likewise sees 2 12—14 as a prophetic admonition consisting of the following elements: a call to national lament (2 12), a *persönliche Glaubensentscheidung* (13a); the summonses in 12—18a are based on a promise of salvation (2 14), which in turn rests on a *Heilszusage*[29] formulated as a doxology (2 13b). T. M. Raitt[30] is even more emphatic than Wolff in asserting that the prophetic summons to repentance is a *Gattung* in its own right. He regards 2 12—14 as a cultic adaptation[31] of such a summons, and sees this *Gattung* as comprising elements of a messenger formula, an admonition and a promise.

As we can see, although there is no perfect consensus on terminology and related matters, by and large it is agreed that the *Gattung* of 2 12—14 is that of a summons to repentance.

The *Gattung* of 2 15—17 should perhaps be approached somewhat differently. Robinson,[32] who regarded the previous section as a liturgy of repentance sees 2 15—18 as an injunction to attend a gathering of repentance. Deden[33] and Thompson[34] make no distinction between the *Gattung* of the

---

[22] IB 6, 747.
[23] Op. cit., 98.
[24] Sellin, op. cit., 161.
[25] BKAT XIV/2, 47ff.
[26] Ibid.
[27] Der Aufruf zur Volksklage, ZAW 76 (1964), 56.
[28] Prophetie und Apokalyptik bei Joel, Theologia Viatorum 10 (1965/6), 238.
[29] Cf. also M. Bič, op. cit., 59.
[30] The prophetic summons to repentance, ZAW 83 (1971), 31.
[31] Raitt, op. cit., 36; Allen, op. cit., 77 strongly agrees with Raitt.
[32] Op. cit., 63.
[33] Op. cit., 96.
[34] Op. cit., 747.

two sections, but Rudolph[35] gives 2 15—17 a slightly different slant (from the summons to repent of 2 12—14) by calling it a summons to a day of fasting.

Wolff once again makes a valuable contribution by defining 2 15—17 as a summons to a national lament or a summons to a *Klagefeier*.[36] Müller[37] uses similar terms and discerns two elements in the summons: the series of *imperatives* (2 15—16), which are so strongly stressed as to forego the customary substantiation; and the cited *lament* in 2 17. The latter element in turn consists of a prayer for divine help and a prayer for deliverance.

L. C. Allen[38] points out that 2 17b in particular has typical elements of the collective lament: "Two petitions are followed by a plaintive question which presents the main basis of the appeal for divine intervention". Ps. 79 4 and 8 presents interesting parallels in this connection.

Although the arguments in favour of describing 2 15—17 as a summons to a national lament are plausible enough, one must stress the difference between, and progression on the summons in 1 5—14:[39] *firstly*, the "congregation" (referred to as ʿăm and qahal in 2 15—17) that is being summoned is described in far greater detail than in 1 14b (ʾîsᵉpu zᵉqenîm kol jošᵉbe haʾaræṣ), specifying that it consists of *elders, children*, even nursing infants (2 16a and b). Even *newly weds* who could plead strong grounds for absence[40] are not excused. The entire people — old and young, every man jack of them — is being summoned. All "parties" to the covenant must attend for the whole community is in peril of judgment.[41] This all encompassing summons to a national lament conveys the cogent relevance of the prophetic message to all the people. Another point to be noted is that behind these pressing injunctions there is the *Unbedingtheit*[42] of God's will.

---

[35] KAT XIII/2, 59.

[36] BKAT XIV/2, 47; cf. also Wolff, ZAW 76 (1964), 50; for a detailed discussion of this *Gattung*, cf. C. Westermann, Struktur und Geschichte der Klage im Alten Testament, ZAW 66 (1954), 44—80, especially 52 ff.

[37] Op. cit., 237.

[38] Op. cit., 83.

[39] Cf. Wolff, BKAT XIV/2, 47 and Rudolph, KAT XIII/2, 59—60.

[40] Cf. e. g. Dtn 20 7 ("And what man is there that has betrothed a woman and has not taken her? Let him go back to his house, lest he die in the battle and another man take her") and Dtn 24 5 ("When a man is newly married, he shall not go out with the army or be charged with any business; he shall be free at home one year, to be happy with his wife whom he has taken").

[41] Allen, op. cit., 82.

[42] Weiser, op. cit., 116.

The second major difference between this summons to lamentation and the one in 1 5—14[43] is that, unlike in 1 14c, the author does not stop at a summons to earnest prayer. In this pericope (cf. 2 17b c d) we have the actual substance of the prayer in which Yahweh's mercy is implored. The basis of this prayer is, of course, divine election[44] (ʿāmmæka-17b; naḥªlatᵉ-ka-17c) with the implication that if the anticipated succour were not forth-coming, Israel — and ultimately Yahweh himself — would become the laughing stock of the nations. H.-P. Müller's[45] comments on the *Gattung* are so important that we shall reproduce them in full: "Von hieraus wird die weitreichende Funktion des ganzen zwischen Gott, Prophet und Volk ge-spannten Geschehens einsichtig: die Klage streckt sich nach der Zuwen-dung Gottes und der daraus folgenden Rettung aus; entsprechend dient der Aufruf zur Klage dazu, die in seiner Begründung gekennzeichnete Not durch die Umkehr des Volkes und das dadurch ermöglichte gnädige Ein-greifen Gottes zu wenden. Insofern Gott hinter der Not wie hinter dem Aufruf steht, spielt sich im Hintergrund beider Kampf Gottes gegen Gott um sein Volk ab. Die Existenz Israels vollzieht sich im Widerspruch des 'offenbaren Gottes' gegen den 'verborgenen Gott' und zwar als die in der prophetischen Anrede erschlossene Möglichkeit des Rufs an jenen gegen diesen".

Thus the two *Gattungen* in this pericope — the *Bußruf* and the sum-mons to national lament — serve to highlight the progression on the earlier pericopes, consisting mainly in the contrast between the earlier crisis and Yahweh's impending wrath, and the subsequent new hopes of mercy and grace.

The text offers no direct clues enabling us to infer anything about the *Sitz im Leben* — either the historical or the cultic *Sitz*.

For a proper understanding of the pericope one must also look into any possible *traditions and other stereotyped material*. In 2 17c one finds the term naḥªlatᵉka[46] which is closely attached with the tradition of the *promise of the land*. Theologically this tradition is based on Yahweh's per-sonal conquest of the land as "commanding officer". Hence the land be-

---

[43] Cf. Rudolph, KAT XIII/2, 59.

[44] Ibid.

[45] Theologia Viatorum 10 (1965/66), 238.

[46] For a discussion of this term, cf. F. Horst, Zwei Begriffe für Eigentum (Verbannung und Heimkehr — W. Rudolph zum 70. Geburtstage), 1961, 135—156; A. Malamat, Mari and the Bible: Some patterns of tribal organization and institutions, JAOS 82 (1962), especially 148 ff.

longs to the Lord and is his naḥᵃlā. In this tradition Yahweh's ownership
and omnipotence usually feature prominently. F. Horst puts it in a nutshell
when he claims that Yahweh's naḥᵃlā in the Old Testament indicates the
"personalen Herrschaftsbereich Gottes".⁴⁷

It is important, however, to establish the context of this tradition in the
present case and to see how it is used. Firstly, note that here naḥᵃlatᵉka parallels ᶜammæka (cf. the structure – 17b and 17c), hence we know that more
is at stake than just the land: the land and the people are an integral entity,
depicted as Yahweh's property. The terms naḥᵃlatᵉka and ᶜammæka could
also be regarded as covenant terminology, and are used to stress the close
relationship between Yahweh and his people.

Secondly, the promise of land tradition is here used in conjunction
with another *conventional motif,* namely that Israel is derided by the nations (17c: lᵉḥærpā). In this pericope and elsewhere this conventional motif
is closely associated with a collective lament.⁴⁸ *The tradition of the promise
of land, in conjunction with the conventional motif ḥærpā, here serve as
grounds for imploring divine intervention on behalf of Israel.*⁴⁹ Hence in
this respect this pericope alters the direction of the *previous* one, which
concerned the approach of the great and terrible day of Yahweh – the people are faced with the dread of his coming. By contrast this pericope is be-
seeching Yahweh to intervene on his people's behalf. *Ultimately it is concerned with Yahweh's reputation. If his naḥᵃlā and his ᶜām are held up to
ridicule, Yahweh himself would be ridiculed and the nations could then as-
sert that he is impotent.*⁵⁰

This pericope contains other conventional material as well, such as the
šûbû ᶜādâ⁵¹ (2 12b) – the repentance or return to Yahweh, a motif that
recurs frequently throughout prophetic literature.⁵² The prophetic call to
return to Yahweh is a summons to Israel to return to its first love, an appeal
deriving from salvation history. In Joel 2 this summons to repentance is
again based on, or at least accompanied by, words of salvation.⁵³

---

⁴⁷ Op. cit., 143.
⁴⁸ Cf. especially Pss 44 14–17; 74 18; 79 4, 12.
⁴⁹ Cf. Keller, op. cit., 132; H.-M. Lutz, Jahwe, Jerusalem und die Völker, 1968, 38; cf. also
Bewer, op. cit., 109.
⁵⁰ Cf. Rudolph, BKAT XIII/2, 60.
⁵¹ For a special discussion on the incidence of this root cf. W. L. Holladay, The root subh in
the Old Testament, 1958, cf. especially 118–156, in particular 141 and 147. Cf. also H. W.
Wolff, Das Thema, "Umkehr" in der alttestamentliche Prophetie, ZThK 48 (1951),
129–148.
⁵² Cf. e.g. Jer 3 21; 18 8; 36 3, 7; Isa 19 22; Am 4 6ff.; Thr 3 40.
⁵³ Wolff, ZThK 48 (1951), 137.

In 2 12b this call to repentance is specified in more detail: bᵉkål-lᵉ-bǎbkæm. Israel must turn to the Lord with its "whole heart", that is totally. This bᵉkål-lᵉbǎbkæm in combination with šûbû is another conventional formula occurring only once in prophetic literature[54], although there are many instances of it in the so-called Deuteronomic history.[55] In 2 13a the call to repentance is defined yet further: wᵉqirᵉ'û lᵉbǎbkæm wᵉ'ǎl-bigᵉdêkæm. It is reiterated that the repentance should not be purely outward, but must be *complete*.

In 13b and c the call to return to Yahweh is substantiated by a hymnic recital of the "attributes" of Yahweh (kî-ḥǎnnûm . . .). This is a conventional *Bekenntnisformel*[56] which also occurs, with minor modifications, elsewhere in the Old Testament.[57] However, Jon 4 2 is the only other instance where the formula is amplified with the expression wᵉniḥam 'ǎl-hara'ā in 2 13c. Joel "takes up this familiar language to explain the surprising about-face from a depiction of Yahweh as dire enemy of his people (2:1–11) to an invitation to repentance (2:12)".[58] Hence the conventional formula serves as a transition from an irate Yahweh to a merciful God.[59] Wolff[60] points out the close thematic correspondence between 2 13c and Jon 4 2. In both cases catastrophe evokes penitence or remorse, which in turn culminates in Yahweh's acceptance of the penitents. We need not elaborate logocentrically on each of the words used to describe Yahweh. It is sufficient to point out that this conventional phrase stresses his gracious long-suffering and loving response to his people's penitence.

In 2 14a there is another conventional formula, mî jôde'ǎ, found mainly in sceptical wisdom literature.[61] In 2 14a, and elsewhere in the Old Testament[62] it is used in the sense of "perhaps" or "possibly".[63] What would its function be in this context? mî jode'ǎ occurs in conjunction with jašûb (the "possible" repentance of Yahweh) and niḥam (penitence). Using jašûb

---

[54] Jer 24 7; cf. also Jer 29 13.

[55] Cf. Dtn 4 29ff.; 30 10; I Sam 7 3; I Reg 8 48; II Reg 23 25; in this last instance this is said of an individual, King Josiah, cf. also Dtn 6 5.

[56] Wolff, BKAT XIV/2, 58.

[57] Cf. Ex 34 6. (For a detailed discussion cf., R. C. Dentan, The literary affinities of Exodus XXXIV 6 f, VT 13 (1963), 34–51; J. Scharbert, Biblica 38 (1957), 130–150; Ps 86 15; Ps 103 8; Ps 145 8; Neh 9 17.

[58] Allen, op. cit., 80.

[59] Rudolph, KAT XIII/2, 58.

[60] Wolff, BKAT XIV/2, 58.

[61] Wolff, BKAT XIV/2, 59; cf. Koh 2 19; 6 12; Jer 17 9.

[62] Jon 3 9; II Sam 12 22.

[63] Cf. also Am 5 15; Zeph 2 3; Thr 3 29 and Ex 32 30 where "perhaps" is used.

establishes a clear connection with the penitence of the people (šubû — 12b and wᵉšûbû — 13b). The mî jôdeʿă ("who knows" or "perhaps") indicates that there is no direct, causal connection between the people's penitence and Yahweh's response. Rudolph rightly observes:[64] „Auch menschliche Reue und Buße schafft kein Anrecht auf die Vergebung, Gott bleibt stets souverän und läßt sich in seiner Freiheit nicht einschränken". Hence penitence is not a means of pressurizing Yahweh into an automatic response, nor can his freedom be trammeled by it. He retains his sovereignty.[65] Thus the relation between Yahweh's impending wrath (2 1—11) and his "possible" mercy is somewhat tense,[66] albeit hopeful as well. From the overall[67] textual context of răḥûm it is obvious that Yahweh is not depicted as a feeble, fickle being. The anthropomorphism therefore indicates that he is not a petrified, lifeless God, but a loving God in a living relationship with his people.

Clearly, then, the author of Joel was not writing in a vacuum but drew freely on traditional material. His way of using and actualizing this material, however, is very much his own.

The *redaction history* of the pericope relates closely to that of the book as a whole. Some scholars believe that 2 12—14 originally followed directly on 2 9[68] or even after 1 20[69]. The latter group argue that the so-called apocalyptic redactor subsequently inserted 2 1—11 in between. T. H. Robinson,[70] on the other hand, claims that 2 12—14 is a fragment from a liturgy of penitence. These viewpoints can hardly be justified from a study of the text and usually derive from the exegete's own subjective presuppositions. Our analysis has shown that 2 12—17 constitutes a unit as regards both form and content, and that it iš moreover indissolubly linked to the preceding pericopes, which it intensifies. Hence Wolff[71] sums it up very aptly: "Somit hat 2:1—17 seinen Ort nicht nur literarisch, sondern sachlich hinter Kap. 1. Die Folge ist unumkehrbar."

Our exegesis as a whole enables us to conclude as follows on 2 12—17 *with special reference to the theology of the pericope:* The passage opens with the familiar nᵉʾum-jhwh formula, the only instance where it is used in Joel. This adds special emphasis to the call to repentance in that Yahweh

---

[64] KAT XIII/2, 59.
[65] Cf. W. S. Prinsloo, Jahwe die Vrymagtige, (diss.) 1976.
[66] Weiser, op. cit., 114.
[67] Deden, op. cit., 100.
[68] Cf. Bewer, op. cit., 104—105.
[69] Cf. E. Sellin, op. cit., 161.
[70] Op. cit., 63.   [71] BKAT XIV/2, 49.

pronounces it in the first person. By using this formula the author shows that the summons comes not from him, but from Yahweh.[72] Thus Yahweh personally inaugurates the crucial turning point in history;[73] he takes the initiative by starting the dialogue that leads to repentance. The n^e°um-jhwh formula is preceded by w^{e}găm-°ăttah, indicating a progression on the preceding pericope: even though Yahweh's wrathful day of reckoning is at hand, there is still hope.

In 12b and 13a the words of God are specified more closely by a passionate call to repentance. The accent is on a "turning" to *Yahweh* (°ădâ). The repetition of the imperatives stresses the urgency of the appeal. The four repetitions of the preposition b^e spells out the exact nature of the repentance: it must be *wholehearted* (b^{e}kål-l^{e}băbkæm), but must be palpably expressed in cultic worship (b^{e}şôm, b^{e}b^{e}kî, b^{e}misped). Yet it must be *not a superficial*, but a sincere and heartfelt repentance. This summons implies, "... eine Umorientierung des ganzen Menschen und seiner Lebensrichtung".[74] The call to repentance is manifestly grounded in the will of Yahweh.

Yahweh's discourse ends in 13a, but the prophet himself takes up the call to penitence in 13b (šûbû), reinforcing its seriousness. As second "witness" the prophet pursues matters further: he specifies the nature of the conversion as a turning to Yahweh. Yahweh is not a stranger, but is °ælo-hêkæm. He has a claim to his people.

The prophet's call to repentance is substantiated (kî) in 13b (second half line) and 13c by a conventional hymnic credal formula strikingly portraying Yahweh's love, grace and mercy. The possibility of repentance does not lie with the people – it is grounded wholly in the grace of Yahweh. The hymnic manner in which Yahweh is depicted underscores his greatness and power.

Another important point is the progression on the preceding pericope. By contrast with the *Alarmbefehl* (2 1–11) and the concomitant imminence of Yahweh's coming, we have here a call to repentance based on Yahweh's mercy. Thus this pericope effects a transition between an irate and gracious God. Looking back on 2 1–11 one realizes that the ominous day of Yahweh was not designed to destroy the people but – as emerges in this pericope – to bring them to repentance, to return to Yahweh. Weiser[75] puts it

---

[72] Kapelrud, op. cit., 81.

[73] Wolff, BKAT XIV/2, 57.

[74] H. W. Wolff, Die Botschaft des Buches Joel, (Theologische Existenz Heute 109), 1963, 25.

[75] Op. cit., 115.

vividly when he says that the crisis and catastrophe are Yahweh's hand reaching out to his people. He waits expectantly to see whether they will accept his hand so that bane may turn into blessing, or whether they will reject his mercy and catastrophe turn into judgment.

Our analysis showed that 13b and c constitute a sort of *nexus* between *Yahweh's discourse* (12b/13a) and the ensuing description of Yahweh's possible response (14a/b). A remarkable word play is used to describe the summons to the people (šubû-12b; šûbû-13b) and Yahweh's response (jašub-14a). Note however, that the call to the people is expressed in unconditional imperatives, whereas Yahweh's response is rendered in the imperfect. This, and the additional fact that the conventional interrogative particle mî jôde°ă is used, clearly indicate that there is no causal connection between the people's repentance and Yahweh's response. Yahweh cannot be manipulated or pressurized by their repentance, nor can his freedom be trammeled by it. Human repentance does not entitle man to automatic forgiveness. Hence there is a certain polarity between Yahweh's imminent wrath and his gracious intervention. Stichs 14a/b arouse the *expectation* of Yahweh's blessing and forgiveness. The striking repetitions of words and phrases from earlier pericopes (cf. discussion above) are a deliberate indication of the hope raised in this pericope that Yahweh will extend his blessing and give his people a fresh chance of life (14a/b). One could say the same about the marked correspondence between 2 1 and 2 15a (tiqᵉ°û šôpar bᵉṣij-jôn). The former is an *Alarmbefehl*, a summons to prepare for Yahweh's imminent coming; the latter is a summons to flee to Yahweh.

Obviously the anthropomorphism in 14a is not meant to depict Yahweh as a fickle being, but rather indicates that he is a God who has a living relationship with his people.

Chapter 2 15–17 is a summons to national lament, yet it differs in certain important respects from the earlier one in 1 5–14:

(i) The congregation is described in far greater detail (cf. 15b/16a with 1 14a). The call is to the entire nation – young and old, nursling and greybeard; even newly weds are not exempt. The whole community is called and none exempted. The string of imperatives affirms the urgency of the summons; behind these pressing injunctions is the inexorable will of Yahweh.

(ii) Another difference is, that whereas 1 14c merely issues the injunction to pray to Yahweh, the second pericope renders the substance of the supplication for divine aid. The tradition of the promise of land (naḥᵃ-latᵉka) is used as ground for imploring Yahweh to intervene yet again on behalf of his people so that they will not be held up to derision by foreign nations. Ultimately it is a matter of Yahweh's own reputation, for if his property (naḥᵉlatᵉka, ʿăm) is held up to scorn it puts Yahweh himself in disrepute.

To sum up: The threatening crisis of the preceding pericope is changed in the hope that Yahweh will be merciful and intervene on his people's behalf. The change is effected through penitence, but the result of such penitence is not automatic. In the final analysis the change is effected, not through the people's cultic rites, but through Yahweh's free act of divine grace.

VII. 2 18–27

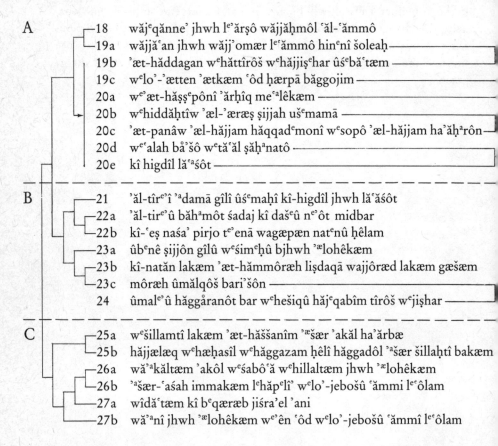

A
- 18   wăjᵉqănneʾ jhwh lᵉʿărṣô wăjjăḥmôl ʿăl-ʿammô
- 19a   wăjjăʿan jhwh wăjjʾomær lᵉʿammô hinᵉnî šoleaḥ
- 19b   ʾæt-hăddagan wᵉhăttîrôš wᵉhăjjiṣᵉhar ûśᵉbăʿtæm
- 19c   wᵉloʾ-ʾætten ʾætkæm ʿôd ḥærpā băggojim
- 20a   wᵉʾæt-hăṣṣᵉpônî ʾărḥîq meᵉᵃlêkæm
- 20b   wᵉhiddăḥtîw ʾæl-ʾæræṣ ṣijjah ušᵉmamā
- 20c   ʾæt-panâw ʾæl-hăjjam hăqqadᵉmonî wᵉsopô ʾæl-hăjjam haʾăḥᵃrôn
- 20d   wᵉʿalah băʾšô wᵉtăʿăl ṣăḥᵃnatô
- 20e   kî higdîl lăᵉᵃśôt

B
- 21   ʾăl-tîrᵉʾî ʾᵃdamā gîlî ûśᵉmaḥî kî-higdîl jhwh lăᵉᵃśôt
- 22a   ʾăl-tîrᵉʾû băhᵃmôt śadaj kî dašᵉû nᵉʾôt midbar
- 22b   kî-ʿeṣ naśaʾ pirjo tᵉʿenā wagæpæn natᵉnû ḥêlam
- 23a   ûbᵉnê ṣijjôn gîlû wᵉśimᵉḥû bjhwh ᵉᵃlohêkæm
- 23b   kî-natăn lakæm ʾæt-hămmôræh liṣdaqā wajjôræd lakæm gæšæm
- 23c   môræh ûmălqôš bariʾšôn
- 24   ûmalᵉʿû hăggăranôt bar wᵉhešiqû hăjᵉqabîm tîrôš wᵉjiṣhar

C
- 25a   wᵉšillamtî lakæm ʾæt-hăššanîm ᵉᵃšær ʾakăl haʾărbæ
- 25b   hăjjælæq wᵉhæḥasîl wᵉhăggazam ḥêlî hăggadôl ᵉᵃšær šillaḥtî bakæm
- 26a   wăᵉᵃkăltæm ʾakôl wᵉśabôʿă wᵉhillaltæm jhwh ᵉᵃlohêkæm
- 26b   ᵉᵃšær-ʿaśah immakæm lᵉhăpᵉlîʾ wᵉloʾ-jebošû ʿammi lᵉʿôlam
- 27a   wîdăʿtæm kî bᵉqæræb jiśraʾel ʾani
- 27b   wăᵉᵃnî jhwh ᵉᵃlohêkæm wᵉʾên ʿôd wᵉloʾ-jebošû ʿammî lᵉʿôlam

The demarcation of this pericope poses a number of problems, yet there are sufficient grounds to regard 2 18–27 as a demarcated pericope. By contrast with the prayer immediately preceding it, in which the priests are the subject and Yahweh is addressed in the second person, here the subject changes. Yahweh's acts are described. As opposed to the preceding national lament (see discussion above), from 2 18 onwards we have a promise of salvation. Then, at 3 1a, there is a conventional introductory formula (wᵉ-hajah ʾaḥᵃrê-ken) ushering in a new pericope.

Both the unity of this pericope and its strophal division will emerge clearly from our discussion of its structure (see below). C. A. Keller[1] advances an interesting argument to substantiate the unity of 2 18—27. He calls it a type of antiphonic chant ("de cantique antiphoné") between Yahweh and the prophet. The *prophet* announces the introduction (2 18), to which *Yahweh* responds (2 19—20); the *prophet* replies with a hymn (2 21—24), and *Yahweh* answers with a final promise of salvation (2 25—27). Although the proposition is tempting, there are no incontrovertible proofs of such an antiphony. To be consistent one would have to inquire whether the preceding and succeeding pericopes could not also form part of the antiphonic chant.

The unity of the pericope should rather be sought at a different level, such as the striking repetition of lexemes and phrases: 20e (kî higdîl lăʿᵃśôt) recurs at 21. The verb natăn is conspicuously used twice with Yahweh as its subject (19c: wᵉloʾ-ʾætten and 23b: kî natăn).

The stereotyped formula (dagan, tîrôš, jiṣʿhar) from 19b recurs in much the same form at 24. The striking verb śbʿ (śᵉbăʿtæm, 19b and śabôʿă, 26a) also features twice. The content of 2 18—27 is also unified in that all of it consists of promises of salvation to Yahweh's people.

Although the arguments in favour of the unity of the pericope are plausible enough, the function of 2 18—27 — and of 2 18 in particular — needs to be examined within the overall context of the book of Joel. Many exegetes regard 2 18 as the turning point[2] of the book, dividing it into two major sections: 1 1—2 17 and 2 18—4 21.[3] Wolff[4] also claims that 2 18 "bringt den entscheidenden Umschwung im Joelbuch". Basically it is argued that 2 18ff. proclaims salvation as opposed to the doom preceding it; that it describes in positive terms that which has hitherto been depicted negatively; that 2 18ff. recounts God's promises to his people.

True as all these contentions are, it is nonetheless doubtful whether one could call 2 18 a turning point or *Umschwung. Firstly,* it would seem that the classical historical-critical model which devides the book into two major sections[5] unduly influenced the demarcation of its pericopes. *Secondly:* although 2 18—27 constitutes a pericope, the break with the preceding

---

[1] Op. cit., 133—134.
[2] G. W. Ahlström, op. cit., 132.
[3] Cf. e. g. C. A. Keller, op. cit., 102.
[4] BKAT XIV/2, 67.
[5] Cf. B. Duhm, ZAW 31 (1911), 187. Duhm regards 2 18—4 21 as an apocalyptic *Ergänzerarbeit* written in prose.

one is by no means as emphatic as is often assumed. The promise of salvation in this pericope is not a new element representing a break. As we have
shown, the preceding pericope (2 12—17) already raised the hope that Yahweh will show mercy and intervene on his people's behalf. In this respect,
therefore, there is no break with the previous pericope but rather a development on it. Just as each pericope has been a progression on the preceding
ones, so 2 18—27 is another link in this chain which culminates in a crescendo at the end of the book. The fact that 2 18—27 continues to elaborate on
its predecessors is also borne out by the following. In 2 17b the speakers are
the priests (jᶜomᵉrû), who request Yahweh wᵉᵊăl-titten naḫᵃlatᶜka lᶜḥærpā
(17c). 2 19 is Yahweh's response: wăjjăᶜan wajjᵓomær ... *Inter alia* Yahweh
promises his people wᵉloᵓ-ᵓætten (19c). The "perhaps" of 2 14ff. (mî jodeᶜă)
is fulfilled in 2 18ff.[6] By means of conspicuously repeated lexemes (cf. 2
17c, lᶜḥærpā ... goĵim, with 19c, ḥærpā băggojim) this pericope is linked
with the preceding one.

Thus the notion of a completely new section of the book starting at 2
18 does not hold water.

2 18 is in fact the fulfilment of the hope raised in the preceding pericope. 2 18ff. is not unexpected: the ground was prepared in the previous
pericope.

Several other exegetes have different views on the place and function of
2 18 and the exact beginning of this pericope. A. Merx[7] regards 2 18 — and
actually 2 19 as well — as a continuation of the jussives of the preceding
passage. He vocalizes the verbs as *waw* copulative instead of the Massoretic
waw consecutive. As a result Merx believes that everything from 2 19 onwards, up to the end of Joel, forms part of the priestly prayer starting at 2
17.

K. Budde[8] comments thus on the view that 2 18 represents a definite
break: "Ganz so einfach, wie es nach dieses Worten scheint, liegen die
Dinge nun wohl doch nicht." Like Merx, Budde vocalizes the verbs in 2 18
as jussives, but he has the words of salvation start at 2 19. In Merx's view
the break comes between 2 18 and 2 19.[9]

---

[6] H.-P. Müller, op. cit., 239.

[7] A. Merx, Die Prophetie des Joel und ihre Ausleger von den ältesten Zeiten bis zu den Reformatoren, 1879, 38 and 90ff.

[8] Der Umschwung in Joel 2, OLZ 22 (1919), 104.

[9] Cf. Merx, op. cit., 106—107; cf. T. H. Robinson, op. cit., 63; Sellin, op. cit., 162 and M.
Bič, op. cit., 65—66 who regards 2 18 as part of the preceding prayer and starts the new
pericope at 2 19. Cf. also S. B. Frost, Old Testament Apocalyptic, 1952, 105.

Bewer,[10] on the other hand, sees no break either between 2 17 and 2 18 or between 2 16 and 2 17. To his mind the pericope starts at 2 15. To justify his position Bewer is compelled to vocalize the verbs of 2 15 ff. not as imperatives but as perfects.

There are two objections against all the foregoing arguments.[11] The first is the transmitted Massoretic text, and the second the fact that 2 18 speaks of Yahweh in the third person whereas 2 17 addresses him in the second person. Thus we espouse the view that the pericope commences at 2 18.

It has been pointed out that 2 18—27 is an intensification of the preceding pericope. By the same token one can say that it culminates in the next pericope. The stereotyped introductory formula (wᵉhajah ʾaḥᵃrê-ken 3 1) not only heralds the start of a new pericope, but also links the two together. The expression wᵉhajah ʾăḥᵃrê-ken undoubtedly refers to something new, but it also harks back to the preceding section and assumes familiarity with it.

Let us next consider the *text-critical*[12] problems of our demarcated pericope 2 18—27. The first problem occurs in 2 20a, namely hăṣṣᵉpônî. K. Budde[13] writes that it is "... eines der schwersten Rätsel, die der Wortlaut der Kleinen Propheten uns aufgibt." A. S. Kapelrud[14] maintains: "In the interpretation of the Book of Joel הצפוני has been a much-contested word, and many interpreters regard it as the very focus in which the different conceptions are refracted." This, rather than text-critical reasons is probably why so many textual emendations have been suggested.[15]

---

[10] Op. cit., 107 ff.

[11] Cf. Rudolph, KAT XIII/2, 62—63; Wolff, BKAT XIV/2, 67.

[12] Only major text-critical problems are discussed here. For minor ones cf. BHS and BHK³ ad loc.

[13] "Der von Norden" in Joel 2, 20, OLZ 22 (1919), 1.

[14] Op. cit., 93.

[15] Cf. i. a. M. Bič, op. cit., 67 and Kapelrud, 93—94 for a detailed discussion of the problem. Important suggestions include K. Budde, "Der von Norden" in Joel 2 20, OLZ 22 (1919), 1—5, after emendating the text to וְהַצָּפוֹן יַרְחִיק הִילֵק מֵעֲלֵיכֶם concludes that this text is referring simply to the north wind (הַצָּפוֹן). Sellin, op. cit., 165 initially suggests emendating the text to צְבָאִי ("my army"), but then produces a new idea (ibid.), namely הַצַּפְצְפוֹנִי. He infers this from a verb צָפַף, meaning "girren, zirpen, schwirren", which Sellin claims describes the noise of locusts in retreat. Sellin's proposal is unacceptable. He is not only creating a new *hapax legomenon*, but his proposition is not supported by textual evidence. It says much that the LXX also renders this text literally: ἀπὸ βορρᾶ ἐκδιώξω ἀφ᾽ ὑμῶν.

Here a hermeneutic problem has resulted in attempts at textual emendation: this is of course not sound practice. Consequently we shall accept hăṣṣ\ʿpônî, despite the hermeneutic problems it raises.[16]

The next major text-critical problem concerns ʾæt-hămmôræh liṣdaqā (23b) and môræh (23c). Here too the text-critical difficulties appear to have arisen from hermeneutic problems. The question is whether môræh (23b) should be translated as "early rain" or as "teacher". Either way there are problems: môræh is not the usual Old Testament word for "early rain".[17] Besides, the combination of môræh (if rendered with "early rain") and ṣ\ʿdaqā poses fresh exegetical problems. Translated as "teacher", môræh fits in well with ṣ\ʿdaqā, but "teacher of righteousness" seems to accord ill with the context since the immediate framework is that of concrete, earthly blessings. The problem is compounded by the repetition of môræh in 23c. As we have shown, these exegetical questions have given rise to various text-critical changes and proposals.[18]

---

[16] When we discuss the text further, we shall return to the meaning of ṣ\ʿpônî.

[17] Only in Ps 84 7 does it have the meaning of "rain".

[18] BHS suggests that 23b could possibly be read simply as kî natăn lakæm ʾæt gæšæm. BHK³ regards liṣdaqā as an addition but does not justify this in any way. The LXX renders with βρώματα ("food"), but the LXX probably reads something other than môræh in the Hebrew text (cf. Kapelrud, op. cit., 114; G. W. Ahlström, Hammôreh liṣdāqāh in Joel II 23, SVT 17 (1969), 25). The rendering is accepted by Bewer, op. cit., 115, and Wolff, BKAT XIV/2, 65. The Vulgate, Targum and Symmachus interpreted môræh as the participial hifil of jrh (to teach, to instruct) and translate môræh in combination with liṣdāqā as "teacher of righteousness". This rendering appears to be fairly popular (cf. e. g. L. H. van der Meiden, De Vertaling van het woord môreh in Joël 2:23, GTT 51 (1951), 137–139; cf. also Weiser, op. cit., 113. Ahlström SVT 17 (1969), 25–36 basically agrees by interpreting môræh as a title and regarding it as an oblique promise of a new Davidic leader. This rendering, "teacher of righteousness", became customary in Jewish circles (cf. e.g. C. Roth, The teacher of righteousness and the prophecy of Joel, VT 13 (1963), 91–95; I. Rabinowitz, The guides of righteousness, VT 8 (1958), 391–404; J. Weingreen, The title moreh sedek, JSS VI (1961), 162–174; R. Meyer, Melchisedek von Jerusalem und moresedek von Qumran, SVT 15 (1966), 228–239).

Sellin, op. cit., ad loc., tries to solve the problem with a different vocalization: he vocalizes the nota accussitivi ʾæt as ʾôt, then renders it with "Denn er hat euch 'ein Zeichen' gegeben, das Gerechtigkeit lehrt, …". Sellin's solution is accepted by Rudolph, KAT XIII/2, 67 and Deden, op. cit., 104 ("Jahweh heeft hun een teken gegeven, dat gerechtigheid leert").

The next alternative is to leave the text unchanged and render môræh with "early rain". Once again there are several supporters, such as Thompson, IB 6, 751; Kapelrud, op. cit., 115 ("The fact that מרה has this identical meaning in Ps. 84:7, proves that it is not unique in our passage"); Robinson, op. cit., 64; M. Bič, op. cit., 75; Allen, op. cit., 92–93; O. R. Sellers, A possible Old Testament reference to the teacher of righteousness, IEJ 5 (1955), 93–95.

After considering all the arguments we can find no decisive reasons for tampering with the Massoretic text, which is therefore retained in this instance as well. Problems not of a text-critical nature will be dealt with when we come to the detailed exegesis.

There are a few other text-critical problems,[19] but since they do not vitally affect matters they will not be discussed here.

Next we come to the *structure* of this pericope. Because of the correspondence in their subjects 18 and 19a are linked. Yahweh is indicated as the subject no fewer than four times (wăjᵉqănneʾ, wăjjăḥmôl-18; wăjjăʿan, wajjʾomær-19a), thereby greatly accentuating his works. The effect is enhanced by the two incidences of the name of Yahweh (18 and 19a). The third person pronominal suffixes of 18 (ʾărṣô and ʿammô) are repeated in 19a (ʿammô). These suffixes indicate Yahweh's proprietary rights as well as his close association with his land and his people. The parallel incidence of ʾărṣô and ʿammô in 18 is striking. The second part of 19a up to the end of 20e is Yahweh's direct speech following wajjʾomær in 19a. From 21 onwards Yahweh is no longer the speaker but the subject of discussion. Thus *18—20e* emerges as a clearly defined pericope section or strophe.

The connections of the direct speech are as follows: Obviously first person singular verbs will occur frequently in Yahweh's direct speech (ʾætten-19c; ʾărḥîq-20a; hiddăḥtîw), once again stressing his acts. The second person plural suffix also crops up several times, ûśᵉbăʿtæm-19b; ʾætten-19c; meʿᵃlêkæm-20a), indicating the recipients of Yahweh's munificence (Israel).

The second môræh in 23c obviously creates a further dilemma. Deden, op. cit., 104 believes that the final m of the preceding word (gæšæm) was duplicated and mistakenly appended to the beginning of jôræh, making it môræh. Rudolph, op. cit., 62 would like to read jôræh instead of môræh, as is done by 34 mss. He believes that môræh in 23c does not mean "rain" but was written incorrectly on the basis of the môræh in 23b.

After considering the above arguments and the textual evidence there appear to be no decisive arguments for changing the text. It would seem to be another case of hermeneutic problems leading to textual emendation. Exegetical presuppositions (for instance the tendency towards a messianic interpretation of this text) also enter into it. The context seems to suggest associating môræh with rain. The fact that the word does not mean rain anywhere else in the Old Testament (with the possible exception of Ps 84 7) is no reason to argue that it cannot have this meaning in Joel 2 23. Word-play — a style device not uncommon in Joel — would appear to have influenced the choice of the word. Possibly the author's intention with this word-play was to stress that Yahweh was personally effecting all these material blessings.

[19] Cf. BHS and BHK³ ad loc. and the discussions in major commentaries.

Line 19b is closely linked with the latter part of 19a − in fact, the two form a single colon: 19b has no verb and the *nota accusativi* (ˀæt-hǎddagan) depends on the verbal part of 19a (hinᵉnî šoleaḥ). hinᵉnî at once focuses attention on Yahweh's acts. The participle šoleaḥ (19b) indicates that Yahweh is just about to[20] send, to intervene. The deliberate positioning of ˀæt-hǎddagan in 19b accentuates the specific gifts he is sending. Line 19c is antithetically linked with 19ab: lines 19a and b state positively what Yahweh will be doing, whereas 19c as emphatically states what he will not be doing.

In 20a/b/c Yahweh remains the subject, but there is a new object (hǎṣṣᵉpônî). The three stichs are syntactically linked by the first person singular hifil verb forms used to describe Yahweh's acts (ˀǎrḥîq-20a; hiddǎḥtîw-20b). To indicate the object (hǎṣṣᵉpônî) the third person masculine singular suffixes are repeated in 20b (hiddǎḥtîw) 20c (panâw, sopô). Within the group of stichs 20a−c, b and c are even more closely linked, forming a single colon by virtue of the absence of a verb in c which renders it dependent on b. Both stichs moreover contain the aforementioned third person masculine singular suffixes. The preposition ˀæl indicating the threefold eviction of the ṣᵉpônî, also occurs in both stichs.

In 20d the subject changes to boˀš and ṣǎhᵃnā. The synonym parallelism serves an emphatic purpose. The fact that the stench and foul smell emanate from the ṣᵉpônî is evident from the third person masculine pronominal suffixes (bǎˀšô, ṣǎhᵃnatô). Line 20c connects with 20d since the causal kî gives the reason for the events in 20d and, by implication, for all Yahweh's earlier acts. The context as a whole makes it clear that higdîl lǎᶜᵃšôt (20e) refers to the actions of the ṣᵉpônî. His self aggrandisement (higdîl) and hubris are the reasons for Yahweh's actions against him.

The combination 20a b c is linked with 20d/e. As far as content goes the criterion is the common factor, namely Yahweh's action against the ṣᵉpônî. Lines 20a b c d e are logically connected with the preceding stichs since they form part of the same direct speech.

A final point about this pericope section is the striking three repetitions of the *nota accusativi* (19b, 20a and 20c). The prominent position of the particle is probably to accentuate Yahweh's acts yet more strongly.

The next pericope section is 2 21−24. From verse 25 Yahweh ceases to be the topic of discussion and resumes speaking in the first person. 21 and 22a are closely linked by the repetition of ˀǎl-tîrᵉˀî. Lines 22a and 22b are even more closely connected in that the two form a single colon. The causal kî in 22b, in conjunction with the kî in 22a, substantiate the summons in

---

[20] Deden, op. cit., 102.

22a (ʾăl-tirᵉʾû). The first jussive (ʾăl-tîrᵉʾî-21) is followed by two positive imperatives (gîlî, śᵉmaḥî) and a substantiation. The jussive and imperatives are addressed to ʾᵃdamā and are substantiated by Yahweh's acts (kî — higdîl jhwh lăᶜᵃśôt). Note the deliberate contrast between the kî higdîl lăᶜᵃśôt in 20e and the kî higdîl jhwh lăᶜᵃśôt of 21. In the former instance it is used in *malem partem* as grounds for Yahweh's punitive action.

The second jussive (ʾăl-tirᵉʾû-22a) is addressed to the beasts of the field (băhᵃmôt śadaj). By contrast with 21 it is not followed by imperatives, but by a twofold substantiation.

Line 23a hits one in the eye due to the prominent position of bᵉnê ṣij-jôn. The affirmative *waw* at the start of the line strengthens the emphasis yet further.[21] Hence it is made very clear that the parties addressed are the bᵉnê ṣijjôn. Hence these parties are ranked in a clearly ascending order: first the earth (ʾᵃdamā), then the beasts (băhᵃmôt) and finally the sons of Zion. In 23a the imperatives are the same as those used in 21 (gîlû, śimᵉḥû). They are told quite explicitly to rejoice: bjhwh ʾælohêkæm. As in the previous two instances, this is followed by a substantiation via a causal kî. The reason for the summons to rejoice is the action of Yahweh (kî natăn). Line 23c has no verb and depends on 23b, so that these two stichs together provide the substantiation for 23a, while 24 (*waw* plus perfect) tells the result of 23b and c. Lines 23a—24 are logically connected with the preceding 21—22b.

The final strophe of this pericope is 25a—27b. At 25a we once again have Yahweh speaking in the first person singular (wᵉšillamtî). Syntactically 25a and b are linked in that b continues the relative clause started in 25a. The content of both stichs is a description of the locusts. Note in passing the significant way in which the locusts are described in more detail than the army (ḥêli) sent by Yahweh. Another significant point is that Yahweh is the one that sent not just the wheat, wine and oil (19a: hinᵉnî šoleaḥ), but also the locusts (šillaḥti-25b) — hence he is the bringer of judgment and blessing alike.

26a and b are also linked in that 26b is a relative clause (ʾᵃšær) dependent on 26a. At 26a the subject changes (wăʾᵃkăltæm, wᵉhillaltæm) to describe the people's response to Yahweh's action: they will have plenty to eat, but will be expected to praise Yahweh for this. The verb śbᶜ, previously used in 19b, is repeated. The relative clause in 26b serves to describe Yahweh as the one who performed a miracle (lᵉhăpᵉlîʾ) for his people. Yahweh himself speaks again almost parenthetically: wᵉloʾ-jebošû ᶜammi lᵉᶜôlam. The purpose of it all is that his people will never again be put to shame. The

---

[21] Cf. Keller, op. cit., 133 footnote 1.

second person plural verb is continued in 27a (widăʿtæm), thus linking it
with the preceding line.

27b is the climax of this strophe and probably of the entire pericope.
wăᵃnî is emphatically positioned. By assigning such prominence to ᵃnî, the
author effects an anadiplosis with the ᵃnî at the end of stich 27a. In 27b
both the phrase jhwh ᵃelohêkæm from 26a and the expression weloʾ-jebošû
ʿammî leʿôlam from 26b are repeated, naturally lending great emphasis to
the matters in question. Thus 27b is closely linked with the immediately
preceding stichs. As a result 26a—27b connects logically with 25a/b.

The three pericope sections or strophes A (18—20), B (21—24) and C
(25—27) are linked in straight-forward, step-by-step fashion. In A and C
Yahweh is the speaker, in B the prophet once again summons the people.

As regards *metre*, this pericope — like the rest of Joel — shows little
uniformity.[22]

In 2 21—24 there are a few synonym parallelisms, but one must agree
with Wolff[23] that to Joel "die Verarbeitung der Tradition mit seinen ak-
tuellen Anliegen wichtiger ist als dichterische Gestaltung."

The words and phrases from earlier pericopes repeated here also warrant mention. These repetitions are deliberate and serve a specific purpose.
The expression ᵃæt-hăddagan wehăttîrôš wehăjjiṣehar in 19b (cf. also 24) is a
deliberate reference to 1 10b (cf. also 1 7a; 1 11a; 1 12a). In this latter context (1 10ff.) the phrase indicated that basic staple commodities were destroyed and the relationship with Yahweh was disrupted. In the later context it is used in a speech by Yahweh to show that he gives his people boun-
tiful gifts.

In the previous pericope (2 17c) Yahweh is beseeched: weᵉăl-titten na-
hᵃlateka leḥærpā. Here he responds (2 19c) weloʾ-ʾætten ʾætkæm ʿôd ḥærpâ.
This indicates a positive answer to the prayer which Yahweh heard.

1 16b tells how joy and gladness (śimḥā wagîl) are dispelled from the
house of the Lord. In this pericope there is a dual summons to rejoice once
more (2 21, gîlî ûśᵉmahî; 23a, gîlû weśimehû). Hence the lost joy and gladness are restored.

After the destruction (weʾăḥᵃrâw midbăr šᵉmamāh) of 2 3b follow re-
covery and fruitfulness (dašᵉʾû neʾôt midbar-22a). The locusts destroyed everything in 1 4a/b. Now the tables are turned (2 25a b) and the plague has
been arrested. In 2 25b Yahweh refers to ḥêlî hăggadol in terms similar to

---

[22] Cf. e.g. Allen, op. cit., 86—87; Bewer, op. cit., 111, 115, 117; Robinson, op. cit., 63, 64.
[23] BKAT XIV/2, 70.

those of 2 11a (hêlô). Both instances thus indicate that the army was not acting independently of Yahweh, but was in fact under his command.

In 26b and 27b the expression wᵉloʾ-jebošû ᶜammi lᵉᶜôlam is conspicuously repeated. We have pointed out the word-play and prominence of the verb bwš in 1 11a–12c (cf. relevant discussion). In 1 11–12 this verb serves to depict the disaster accompanying the destruction of food and all natural means of survival. In this pericope (2 26b and 27b) it is put into Yahweh's mouth as a promise that his people will never be put to shame again.

These examples all demonstrate that this pericope is the counterpart of 1 2–14. Judgment and destruction have been converted to deliverance and promises of prosperity.

Let us now turn to the *Gattung* of this pericope. Broadly speaking *2 18–20* may be described as an *oracle*. The stereotyped formula wǎjjǎᶜan ...[24] in 2 19a is often used to introduce oracles, more particularly ones that represent answer to prayer. The hinᵉnî (19a) followed by a participle (šoleaḥ) further characterizes this strophe as an *Erhörungsorakel*.[25] This particle (hinᵉnî) is used to focus attention on the ensuing topic – Yahweh's gracious intervention. C. A. Keller[26] calls 2 18–19a "bénédiction" and 2 20a "malédiction". It is probably unnecessary to classify 2 20 as a separate *Gattung* – in fact the judgment pronounced on the ṣᵉpônî should rather be seen as a subsection of the oracle of salvation.

Scholars on the whole agree about 2 21–23. Robinson[27] sees it as a typical psalm of thanksgiving distinguished by the call to rejoice (21, 23a) and the reason for this summons. Sellin[28] calls it a song of thanksgiving, Deden[29] a hymn of thanksgiving and Keller[30] a song or hymn of praise. H.-P. Müller is thinking along similar lines, but specifies the *Gattung* of 2 21ff. and 23ff. as anticipatory songs of praise,[31] distinguished by the fact that Yahweh is referred to in the third person. By "anticipatory" Müller means that God is being praised for the promised deliverance as if it has already happened. The context does not permit us to decide whether the perfects of

---

[24] Cf. e. g. I Sam 7 9; 23 4; Ps 20 2; 22 22; 60 7; 118 5. Cf. also Wolff, BKAT XIV/2, 73; Sellin, op. cit., 164; Deden, op. cit., 102.

[25] Cf. Rudolph, KAT XIII/2, 63; Wolff, BKAT XIV/2, 68; P. Humbert, Problèmes du livre d'Habacuc, 1944, 12.

[26] Op. cit., 134.

[27] Op. cit., 65.

[28] Op. cit., 166.

[29] Op. cit., 117/118.

[30] Op. cit., 134.

[31] Op. cit., 240.

21 ff. should be seen as prophetic[32] or historical[33] perfects. Müller's view is based on the assumption that they are prophetic, but since this point is undecided it would be safer to speak of a song or hymn of praise rather than an anticipatory one. The hymnic character of 2 21—24 is indisputable.

H. W. Wolff must be credited with the interpretation of these hymnic elements as part of a larger *Gattung*. Following J. Begrich,[34] Wolff proves convincingly that the expression 'ăl-tîr^e'rî (21 and 22a) is a cardinal feature of the *Erhörungszuspruch:*[35] this oracle of answered prayer is amplified with hymnic elements[36] which speak of Yahweh in the third rather than in the first person.[37] Hence 2 21—24 is not an isolated hymn but part of an oracle commencing at 2 18. This oracle is resumed in 2 25—27 where Yahweh once more speaks in the first person. This passage culminates in the so-called *Erkenntnisformel*, which has itself been identified as a fixed component of the *Erhörungswort*.[38]

To sum up, the *Gattung* of this pericope could be defined as an *Erhörungswort*, greatly amplified and consisting of diverse elements. It links up neatly with the call to repentance in the preceding pericope. We have no information about the *Sitz im Leben* of this pericope. The claim that 2 18—27 is inspired by the liturgy of the annual autumnal feast[39] is unsubstantiated. Nor can Müller's view[40] that ". . . hinter ihr (i. e. the words of this pericope — W. S. P.) wird die Institution eines öffentlichen Fastens sichtbar, das aus Anlaß umfassender Kalamitäten je und je ausgerufen werden kann" be accepted.

There are no *traditions* in the strict sense of the word, but M. Bič is quite right when he comments about 2 22—23: "Der Zusammenhang mit der Schöpfungsage 1. Mose ist unverkennbar."[41] The author of Joel uses similar terminology (cf. Gen 1 11; 1 29; 1 24ff.) and the same sequence (earth, beasts, man) as Gen 1. As a result Yahweh's redemptive work in this pericope is depicted as a new *act of creation*. Several other conventional ele-

---

[32] Thus Allen, op. cit., 90.
[33] Deden, op. cit., 103; Rudolph, KAT XIII/2, 63.
[34] Das priesterliche Heilsorakel, ZAW 52 (1934), 81—92: "Das Orakel beginnt gewöhnlich mit den Worten 'fürchte dich nicht'."
[35] BKAT XIV/2, 68. Cf. also Thr 3 57; Isa 41 10, 13, 14; 43 1, 5; 44 2; 51 7; Jer 30 10.
[36] Cf. also Isa 41 14—16.
[37] Cf. also Ps 89 9—14.
[38] Cf. Wolff, BKAT XIV/2, 68 and Isa 45 5ff., 18, 22; 46 9.
[39] Thus Keller, op. cit., 135.
[40] Op. cit., 241.
[41] Op. cit., 73—74. Cf. also Keller, op. cit., 138, footnote 1.

ments can be traced in this pericope. Thus qn' is the verb customarily used to express Yahweh's fervent love for his people.[42] Rudolph[43] puts it in a nutshell: "In קנא steckt ein ebenso blutvoller Anthropapathismus wie in נחם: Es ist die Leidenschaft mit der sich Jahwe für (oder gegen[44]) jemand einsetzt und in der immer ein Stückchen Eifersucht dabei ist, wenn die anderen Völker durch ihren Spott Israel seinem eigenen Gott abspenstig machen wollen." This anthropomorphism vividly reflects the dynamic vitality of the Old Testament concept of God.[45] This is the context within which it introduces Yahweh's gracious intervention on behalf of his people.

We mentioned earlier that hăddagan wᵉhăttîrôš wᵉhăjjiṣᵉhar[46] (19b) is a conventional formula for Palestine's principal agricultural products. Here it serves to indicate that Yahweh is blessing his people abundantly, that the crisis has been arrested and harmony between Yahweh and his people restored. The use of the same formula heightens the contrast between 1 10 and 2 18ff.

The conventional phrase hăṣṣᵉpônî[47] poses distinct problems, but it would be digressing to discuss in full the whole issue concerning the "foe from the north", in inquiry into the original *Sitz im Leben* of the concept ṣapôn, or even the various attempts at establishing the meaning of ṣᵉpônî in 2 20a.[48]

20a indicates that Yahweh will deliver his people from the ṣᵉpônî. From the rest of Joel we know that the crisis was caused by a plague of locusts and an accompanying drought. In 2 1—11 we found that the locusts were described in dramatic hyperbole, implying that far more than a plague of locusts was at stake. In the present context too we are clearly dealing with more than just a locust plague. In the stich immediately before this

---

[42] Cf. also Sach 1 14; 8 2; Isa 9 6; 37 32; II Reg 19 31. For a detailed discussion cf. H. A. Brongers, Der Eifer des Herrn Zebaoth, VT 13 (1963), 269—284.

[43] KAT XIII/2, 63.

[44] Cf. e. g. Ez 5 13; 16 38, 42; 23 25; Ps 79 5.

[45] Weiser, op. cit., 117.

[46] Cf. the discussion of 1 10 above; cf. also Dtn 7 13; 11 14; 28 51; Hos 2 8 (11); Ps 104 15ff.

[47] Cf. e.g. Jer 1 14; 4 6; 6 1; Ez 38 6, 15; 39 2.

[48] For a detailed discussion cf. Kapelrud, op. cit., 93—108; K. Budde, "Der von Norden" in Joel 2, 20, OLZ 22 (1919), 1—5; B. S. Childs, The enemy from the north and the chaos tradition, JBL 78 (1959), 187—198; Wolff, BKAT XIV/2, 73—74; M. Dahood, The four cardinal points in Psalm 75,7 and Joel 2,20, Biblica 52 (1971), 397; J. P. Hyatt, The peril from the north in Jeremiah, JBL 59 (1940), 499—513. Cf. also W. S. Prinsloo, Isaiah 14: 12—15 — Humiliation, Hubris, Humiliation, ZAW 93 (1981), 437, footnote 35 for further literature; H.-M. Lutz, Jahwe, Jerusalem und die Völker, 1968, 23—130.

(19c) we have the conventional formula of Israel being held to scorn by the nations (ḥærpa băggojim, cf. also 2 17c).

In 20b—c where the ṣᵉpônî is described more closely the author is plainly concerned with something greater than a locust plague. We have to concede Kapelrud's point:[49] "... it is obvious that הצפוני transcends the limits of locusts, even though locusts in Joel are in fact the point of departure for the designation." Although it is difficult to determine exactly who or what the ṣᵉpônî is, here it clearly symbolizes[50] the mysterious force which constitutes a threat to Yahweh's people.[51] Since the expression also has mythological connotations, one cannot exclude the possibility that Yahweh is being portrayed as the God who commands all mythological powers as well. At all events, the point is clearly made that he will take the initiative in destroying the forces that imperil his people.[52]

In 2 21 and 23a there is another conventional element namely the word pair gîlî ûśᵉmaḥî.[53] Usually this expression occurs when there is a summons to praise Yahweh for something or other — in this case because he has turned the catastrophe to blessing.

The so-called *Erkenntnisformel* in 2 27a, occurs frequently in the Old Testament, particularly in Ez.[54]

2 27 links up closely with Isa 45 5 ff.[55] as well. Zimmerli[56] demonstrated convincingly that this formula does not occur in isolation but is deeply im-

---

[49] Op. cit., 107; Robinson op. cit., 64 comments further: "So laßt die Bezeichnung der 'Nördliche' hier auch die Heuschrecken als eine über das Maß des Insektes hinausgehende einheimliche Größe erscheinen." Cf. also H.-P. Müller, op. cit., 240: "Naturereignisse werden damit vergeschichtlicht: die Heuschrecken gelten nicht nur allgemein als ein Heer Jahwes 1,6; 2,4—8.11, sondern nun auch speziell als der sagenhafte 'Feind aus dem Norden,' 2,20 ..."

[50] E. Kutsch, op. cit., 93 refers to "Typisierung" in this connection.

[51] If the term has to be used at all one could say that the author is using apocalyptic terms.

[52] H.-M. Lutz, op. cit., 38 points out that it is characteristic of the "northern enemy" tradition that Yahweh uses this foe as an instrument to punish his people. In 2 20, however, the unusual element is that Yahweh turns on his own instrument to destroy it.

[53] Cf. e.g. Ps 14 7; 16 9; 31 8; 31 11; 48 12; 53 7; 96 11; 118 24; I Chr 16 31; Isa 25 9; 66 10; Hab 1 15; Sach 10 7.

[54] Cf. Ez 6 7, 13, 14; 7 4, 27; 11 10, 12; 12 15, 16, 20; 13 9, 14, 21, 23; 14 8; 15 7; 16 22; 20 26, 28, 42, 44; 22 16; 23 49; 24 24, 27; 25 7, 9, 11, 17; 26 6; 28 22, 23, 24; 29 6, 9, 16. Cf. W. Zimmerli, Erkenntnis Gottes nach dem Buch Esechiel, 1954, for a detailed discussion of the formula in Ez as well as the Old Testament as a whole.

[55] For the fact that Yahweh is described as (a) bᵉqæræb jiśra'el and (b) wᵉᵉen 'ôd, cf. respectively (a) Ex 17 7; Num 11 20; 14 4; Dtn 7 21; Hos 11 9; Mi 3 11 and (b) Hos 13 4; Isa 45 5, 18, 22; 46 9.

[56] Op. cit., 12.

bedded in prophetic proclamation in particular. Note that the *Erkenntnis-formel* is almost invariably preceded by a comment on some act of Yahweh: "Die Reihenfolge: Tat Jahwes — Erkenntnis des Menschen, die sich um-kehren läßt, ist für die Beschreibung des Vorganges konstitutiv."[57] This is true of 2 27a as well: the preceding passage describes Yahweh's acts of sal-vation. The immediately preceding stich (26b) tells of the miracle he has performed. These redemptive acts will lead to the acknowledgement that he is (i) in the midst of or with his people, and (ii) the only God.

Clearly, then, the author of Joel made liberal use of conventional mate-rial in this pericope in order to lend more weight to it. The *redaction history* of the pericope also calls for attention. Of course, one's view of it will de-pend on how one sees the redaction history of the book as a whole. Duhm[58] held the well-known view that 2 18–4 21 in its entirety represents an apoca-lyptic "Ergänzerarbeit" written in prose. The redaction history of 2 18–27 as such has elicited considerable comment. H.-P. Müller[59] maintains that in the whole pericope 2 18 alone has a literary character, 2 19–27 representing a preliterary utterance. Neither is there any agreement on the question of whether 2 20 originally formed part of the pericope. Both Bewer[60] and Ro-binson[61] believe that 2 20 (or at least part of it) was added by a later redactor or interpolator. The position of 21–23/4 is likewise disputed. Sellin[62] at-tributes 2 23 to an apocalyptic redactor, citing the absence of rhythm in this verse as confirmation of his view. Robinson[63] claims that 2 21–24 and 2 25–27 were originally two totally unconnected passages subsequently com-bined by a redactor. Bewer[64] calls 2 *21–24* a "poetical insertion" interrupt-ing Yahweh's discourse. Budde[65] too maintains that 2 20 was originally fol-lowed by 2 24, so that 2 *21–23* had not formed part of the original text. Robinson says that 2 *27* was inserted by a redactor who was very much under the influence of Ezekiel. This verse recapitulates the entire passage and the purpose of the redactional addition was to demonstrate that Yah-weh's wondrous deeds were all aimed at one goal: that Israel and all the world should acknowledge that he alone is God.

---

[57] Zimmerli, op. cit., 40.
[58] Duhm, ZAW 31 (1911), 187.
[59] Op. cit., 241.
[60] Op. cit., 111.
[61] Op. cit., 64, cf. also Deissler, NEB, 78.
[62] Op. cit., 168.
[63] Op. cit., 65.
[64] Op. cit., 113.
[65] Der Umschwung in Joel 2, OLZ 22 (1919), 110.

From the above one gathers the only passages whose authenticity have never been disputed are 2 18—19 and 2 25—26. This is not a satisfactory state of affairs, especially if the grounds for regarding certain stichs as redactorial additions are not clearly specified. To see 2 21—24 as a redactional addition simply because — unlike 2 18—20 and 2 25—27 — it refers to Yahweh in the third person seems insufficiently justified. The original author might equally well have intended to convey a deliberate alternation between Yahweh's words and the prophet's. It is extremely difficult to judge, on textual grounds, what are redactional additions. At all events our analysis showed that as regards both form and content the pericope is logically integrated.

Synchronic and diachronic analysis provides a verifiable framework for examining the content of this pericope, with special reference to its *theology*. The chapter reflects a progression on the preceding one — one could even call it a turning point. This is at once evident from the fact that the preceding call to repentance has turned into an *Erhörungswort*. What was a mere hope in the previous pericope is now realized, the "perhaps" of 2 14 has been fulfilled;[66] the prayer has been heard. The pericope heavily emphasizes that it is *Yahweh* who has effected this change. This is particularly evident in 18 and 19a: Yahweh's activity is underscored by making him the subject of no fewer than four consecutive verbs in these lines (wăjᵉqănneʾ, wăjjăḥmol, wăjjăʿan, wăjjʾomær). The emphasis is enhanced by repeating his name in both 18 and 19a. Yahweh's fervent love for his land and his people is clearly reflected by the synonym parallelism in 18. It is remarkable that the land and the people should be mentioned in the same breath, clarifying beyond all doubt that this is the Lord's people (ʿăl-ʿămmô-18; lᵉʿămmo-19a). The focus on Yahweh is accentuated when he himself speaks (19). The particle hinᵉnî followed by the participle (šoleaḥ) draws attention to Yahweh's acts and his immanent presence. In his direct speech in 19b—20c his deeds are continually highlighted by the first person singular verbs (ʾætten-19c; ʾărḥîq-20a; hiddăḥtîw-20b).

In short, the first pericope section heavily stresses the fact that Yahweh is the one to have actualized the hopes and effected the change. It is incontrovertible *that* Yahweh acts, but the direct speech of 19—20c moreover tells *what* he does. In these stichs the contrast between the earlier crisis and Yahweh's acts of salvation is very marked. Yahweh's deeds on behalf of his people are more closely defined in 19b and c:

---

[66] H.-P. Müller, op. cit., 239.

(a) He will once more give them the basic needs of life and primary agricultural products (hăddagan, wᵉhăttîrôš, wᵉhăjjiṣᵉhar) so that they will have enough to eat (ûśᵉbăʿtæm). This is a deliberate reference to 1 10b (cf. also 1 7a; 1 11a; 1 12a) to show that Yahweh has changed the crisis situation to plenty and has normalized relations with his people. Famine has changed to abundance.

(b) It also means that he will not permit his people to be put to shame by other nations. Stich 19c is a direct answer to the prayer in 2 17c.

The destruction of the people's enemies is pre-eminently the topic of 20a—c. Who or what is meant by the ṣᵉpônî is not at all clear: the enemy is a mysterious one for our purpose. The important point is that Yahweh will work the total destruction of this foe (20a b c d). To substantiate this punitive measure we are told that the ṣᵉpônî had been guilty of *hubris* (20c) or self-aggrandisement. From the overall context of the book of Joel one gathers that Yahweh was the one who ordered this enemy against his own people (cf. mainly 2 11a and 2 25a and b). The present stich (20e) shows that Yahweh will punish even his own "punitive instruments" if the latter should exalt himself before Yahweh.

To this promise of salvation Yahweh expects a response, as emerges in 21—24 where the *Erhörungszuspruch* — amplified with hymnic elements — continues. Here Yahweh is no longer the speaker but the topic of discussion. The "congregation" is urgently summoned. Note *how* they are summoned, *who* are summoned and *why*. The summons is conveyed by the jussive ʾăl-tîrᵉʾî in 21, which is repeated in 22a (ʾăl-tîrᵉʾû). The first jussive (21) is followed by a double imperative (gîlî, śᵉmaḥî). The same pattern follows after the second jussive in 23a. These successive injunctions not to fear but to rejoice are in contrast to the "repeated expressions of sorrow"[67] in chapters 1 and 2 (cf. 1 5; 1 8; 1 9; 1 13; 2 13; 2 17), stressing that sorrow has turned to joy. The people who have been deprived of all gladness (cf. 1 16b) are called to rejoice once more.

The hymnic character of this pericope section and particularly the first substantiation, kî-higdîl jhwh lăʿᵃśôt, clearly indicates that Yahweh's deeds are the cause for rejoicing; his redemptive acts have cancelled out the hubris (higdîl) of the ṣᵉpônî (cf. 20e). The summons to rejoice must be bjhwh (23a). It is Yahweh who gives his people the môræh. Thus, like its predecessor, this pericope section is very much theocentric. Yahweh's gracious intervention is the substantiation for the hymnic summons.

---

[67] J. A. Thompson, The use of repetition in the prophecy of Joel, 1974, 105.

There has been a cosmic catastrophe, but now there has been a radical change (cf. the deliberate contrast between this pericope and 1 5—14 in particular, but also 2 1—11) and the whole cosmos (arable land, livestock, humans) has been restored. Thus the *entire cosmos* is called, in ascending order, to praise Yahweh. The unity of the created world with its creator emerges vividly. The earth, the beasts and Yahweh's people join in one great chorale to sing Yahweh's praise. This act of salvation is tantamount to a new act of creation whereby order is restored. Of course, the call to rejoice reaches its crescendo in the summons to the bᵉnê ṣijjôn — Yahweh's relations with his people are also restored. Yahweh is emphatically designated 'ælohekæm (cf. also 26a). To substantiate the summons we are told that Yahweh gave them 'æt-hǎmmôræh liṣdaqā. From the context one must infer that these gifts are straightforward material ones: different words for rain[68] are heaped one on top of the other to indicate the abundance of Yahweh's gift. The exact meaning of liṣdaqā is difficult to determine. It could indicate Yahweh's relationship with his people, so that liṣdaqā would signify that Yahweh will once more give rain in keeping with his ṣᵉdaqā, his loyalty to his people.[69]

The *Erhörungswort* reaches a climax in the final pericope section (2 25—27) where Yahweh is once again the speaker. His acts are again stressed by the first person singular verbs (cf. 25a; 25b), the first person singular pronominal suffix (cf. 25b; 26a; 27b) and the personal pronoun 'ᵃnî (27a and 27b).

Stichs 25a and b depict Yahweh's *acts.* Their *consequences* are described in 26a—27b.

Yahweh's acts consist in compensating his people for the havoc wreaked by the locusts. Thus 25a and b plainly indicate that the catastrophe of 1 4 has been wholly turned to blessing. An important point is that Yahweh was the one who sent the disaster to his people but that it was also he who arrested it. The locusts and the resultant crisis are not distinct from or independent of Yahweh.

Yahweh's intervention has certain consequences:

(a) The people will once more have enough to eat. The theme of 19b is taken up again and the contrast with chapter 1 underscored. Instead of locusts devouring everything Yahweh's people will now have plenty to eat.

---

[68] Cf. discussion above.
[69] Kapelrud, op. cit., 116.

(b) But the amendment of the crisis is not an end in itself. The second half-line of 26a explicitly states that it should culminate in praising the Lord. Those who eat in plenty must know to praise commensurately. Yahweh is the one who brought the change and he must be given thanks for it. He is once again described as ʾælohêkæm and then, in a relative clause, depicted as the one who has dealt wondrously with his people (lᵉhăpᵉliˀ-26b). Wolff[70] aptly comments: "להפליא steht als Adverb, das die ungewöhnliche, nur von Gott selbst her zu verstehende Größe seines Handelns herausstellt." Yahweh did the impossible, the miraculous by changing catastrophe into blessing and bounty.

The refrain (wᵉloˀ-jebošû ʿammi lᵉʿôlam) is an effective response to 2 17c and contrasts with 1 11a—12c: Yahweh's people will never again be put to shame. The ʿammî once again stresses the intimate bond between Yahweh and his people. If ʿammî will not be put to shame again, this is in effect a matter of Yahweh's own reputation: his honour is guaranteed.

The entire pericope culminates in the credal formula in 27a (wîdăʿtæm). The confession is not suspended in a vacuum, but rests solidly on Yahweh's mighty deeds. His acts of salvation lead to a confession, in which he is praised as the one who is with his people (bᵉqæræb). They need not cry to him any more (cf. 1 14), there is a living relationship between Yahweh and his people. He alone is God, there is none beside him. Thus catastrophe culminates in confession.

To recapitulate: In this pericope the hope of the preceding one is actualized. Disaster turns to blessing. Yahweh, who wrought the disaster, also wrought this change. But the change is not an end in itself. It must lead to praising Yahweh and confessing him as the one and only God, active in the midst of his people.

---

[70] Wolff, BKAT XIV/2, 77.

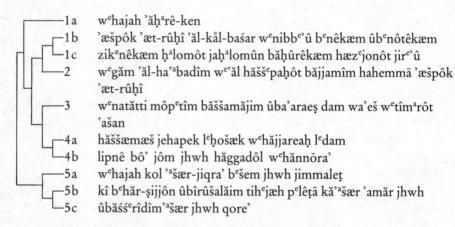

—1a   wᵉhajah ʾăhᵃrê-ken

—1b   ʾæšpôk ʾæt-rûḥî ʿăl-kăl-baśar wᵉnibbᵉʾû bᵉnêkæm ûbᵉnôtêkæm

—1c   zikᵉnêkæm ḥᵃlomôt jaḥᵃlomûn băḥûrêkæm hæzᵉjonôt jirᵉʾû

—2   wᵉgăm ʿăl-ha·ᵃbadîm wᵉᵉʿăl hăššᵉpaḥôt băjjamîm hahemmā ʾæšpôk ʾæt-rûḥî

—3   wᵉnatătti môpᵉtîm băššamăjim ûba·araeṣ dam wa·eš wᵉtîmᵃrôt ʿašan

—4a   hăššæmæš jehapek lᵉḥošæk wᵉhăjjareaḥ lᵉdam

—4b   lipnê bôʾ jôm jhwh hăggadôl wᵉhănnôraʾ

—5a   wᵉhajah kol ʾᵃšær-jiqraʾ bᵉšem jhwh jimmaleṭ

—5b   kî bᵉhăr-ṣijjôn ûbîrûšalăim tihᵉjæh pᵉlêṭă kăʾᵃšær ʾamăr jhwh

—5c   ûbăśśᵉrîdîmʾᵃšær jhwh qoreʾ

The pericope starts with a stereotyped introductory formula, wᵉhajah ăhᵃrê-ken. Although it announces something new, it also refers back to the preceding part.[1] The ʾăhᵃrê-ken focuses attention on events that would only come to pass after the preceding 2 18—27.[2]

The content of 3 1—5 (outpouring of the ruăḥ and portents of the jôm) also sets it apart from the previous pericope. The same applies to its relation to the next pericope (4 1ff.), which starts similarly with a conventional introductory formula, and whose content concerns the proclamation of judgment on hostile nations. Structurally too 3 1—5 is an integral unit, as we shall show.

There are few *text-critical* problems, the only noteworthy one being ûbăśśᵉrîdîm. This applies to syntax and meaning of 5c as a whole.[3]

This hermeneutic problem led to several attempts at textual emendation,[4] but a reading that is difficult to interpret is not sufficient grounds for

---

[1] Kapelrud, op. cit., 7: "Thus it suits well in its place to mark the advance of the prophet's thought."

[2] P. A. Verhoef, op. cit., 57.

[3] For a detailed discussion of the problem, cf. Rudolph, KAT XIII/2, 70—71.

[4] BHS transposes bîrûšalăim from 5b to 5c to read the latter as ûbîrûšalăim śᵉrîdím; cf. also Sellin, op. cit., 171 who maintains that there has been a haplography from the original ûbî-rûsalăim śᵉrîdím, so that jᵉrûsalăim dropped out of 5c. Later jᵉrûsalăim was mistakenly in-

altering the text. We shall therefore retain the Massoretic text and, pending
the detailed exegesis, reserve judgment on the meaning of 3 5c.

The *structure* of this pericope is as follows: 1b is linked with 1c. The
second half line of 1b and 1c as a whole specify the effects of the outpouring
of the ruăḥ, as well as who kâl-baśar is. This is done by means of three statements:

1b^b wᵉnibbᵉʾû bᵉnêkæm ûbᵉnôtêkæm
1c^a zikᵉnêkæm ḥᵃlomôt jaḥᵃlomûn
1c^b băḥûrêkæm hæzᵉjonôt jirᵉʾû

The third person verbs (nibbᵉʾû, jaḥᵃlomûn, jirᵉʾû) and the accompanying second person plural pronominal suffixes (bᵉnôtêkæm, zikᵉnêkæm, ba-
ḥûrêkæm) forge a close syntactic link between the two stichs. In the first
line the *tertium comparationis* would appear to be *sex* (sons and daughters),
and in the second and third lines in 1c, which are parallel as regards form
and metre, the *tertium comparationis* seems to be *age* (băḥur/zaken, that is
young and old).

Thus the first two stichs clearly state that the outpouring of Yahweh's
rûăḥ will result in prophecies, visions and dreams. These "charismatic
gifts" are not the privilege of rare individuals, but will be shared alike by
male and female, young and old.

Stich 2 is closely connected with the preceding verse. The emphatic
wᵉgăm effects a progression on and amplification of the preceding stichs.
The combination 1b—2 manifests an *inclusio* in that it both starts and ends
with ʾæšpôk ʾæt-rûḥî, so that the pericope section is "framed" by the statement that Yahweh will pour out his rûăḥ. This lays the emphasis on Yahweh's act. All the events in 1b—2 are governed by the outpouring of the
rûăḥ. In passing we could note that the aforementioned *inclusio* is marked
by a chiastic structure[5]:

---

serted in 5b. By changing the text thus Sellin seeks to restore the original *parallelismus
membrorum*: bîrûśalăim śᵉrîdîm//bᵉḥăr ṣijjon tihᵉjæh pᵉlêṭā. Sellin is followed by Allen, op.
cit., 102 who substantiates this "conjectural emendation" by citing the following: it solves
the doubtful syntax, "makes the earlier clause conform to the quotation in Obad. 17"; and
restores the parallelism.

Robinson, op. cit., 66 also has difficulty with the bᵉ at śᵉrîdîm and changes it to a verb to
read וְשָׂרְדוּ "und entrinnen werden, die Jahwe ruft." The LXX apparently erroneously read
ûmᵉbăśᵉrîm ("those who bring glad tidings"), but Aquila and Theodotion support the Massoretic text. Rudolph, KAT XIII/2, 66—67 does not alter the text, but believes that śᵉrîdîm
should be interpreted as the parallel of bᵉṣijjôn and jîrûśalăim, whereupon he renders the bᵉ
with "bei den Überlebenden".

[5] Possibly the thesis of Keller, op. cit., 141 to see the whole of the first strophe as an ABCBA
structure testifies to a structuralistic premise.

’æšpôk ’æt-rûḥî ‘ăl ...

w°găm ‘ăl ... w°°ăl ... ’æšpôk ’æt-rûḥi

2 builds on the preceding stichs. By means of the emphatic w°găm, the repetition of the preposition ‘ăl and the prominent position of ‘ăbadîm and š°paḥôt it is pointed out that Yahweh's rûăḥ will be poured out even on slaves, the lowliest in the social order.

Although stich 3 links up with the preceding line and continues Yahweh's speech with its first person singular form (nattătti), there is a change as regards content. Stichs 3 to 4b deal with cosmic change. Within the combination 3–4b, the syntax of 4a/b links them indissolubly into a single colon: lipnê (4b) is the temporal qualification of the verb jehapek. Thus the cosmic disturbances occur *before* the jôm and are portents of it. Stichs 3 and 4a are also closely linked. The signs (môp°tîm) which Yahweh will give in the heavens and on earth (i. e. throughout the cosmos) are more closely specified by. a chiastic[6] structure in the second half line of 3 and in 4a:

Heaven ————————— *earth*
portents on *earth* ———— *portents in the heavens*

From verse 4 onwards the first person lapses (jehapek) and in 4a Yahweh is referred to in the third person (jôm jhwh). Rudolph points out that there is nothing new about the expression Yom Yahweh occurring in a speech by Yahweh.[7] Neither is the apparent interruption of Yahweh's speech sufficient reason to consider these verses a later redactional insertion,[8] it is also not necessary to translate the nifal at jehapek reflexively.[9] In fact, the context rather suggests rendering it as a passive, thus effecting a subtle reference to Yahweh's acts. Most probably there is a deliberate play on words in the ’æšpôk (1b and 2) and jehapek (4a). Yahweh is the subject of both špk and hpk. Note that 3 4b uses terminology similar to that of 2 11c to describe the jôm (cf. also 3 4 with 2 2a and 2 10a and b). One would have to establish whether or not the corresponding terms and the Yom Yahweh tradition serve the same purpose in both contexts.

---

[6] Cf. Keller, op. cit., 143; Wolff, BKAT XIV/2, 81; Rudolph, KAT XIII/2, 73.
[7] Op. cit., 71.
[8] Cf. discussion below.
[9] Cf. Bewer, op. cit., 124: "... the sun will turn *itself* into darkness ...".

At 5a another new pericope section commences (wᵉhajah). In 5 abc it is evident that the kî in 5b should be interpreted causally, so that 5b substantiates the jimmaleṭ in 5a. Syntactically, however, 5c depends on 5b. The tihᵉjæh pᵉlêṭā (5b) is assumed in 5c as well, making the latter the continuation of the substantiation commenced in 5b. Hence ûbăśśᵉrîdîm must be seen as the parallel of bᵉhăr-ṣijjôn and ûbîrûšalăîm,[10] and the waw at the beginning of 5c as affirmative. One can simplify this problematic strophe as follows:

> Everyone who trusts in Yahweh will be saved
>> for *in* Jerusalem and *in* Zion is deliverance
>> [as Yahweh has promised]
> yea *among* the survivors whom the Lord calls.

This pericope section, like 1b–2, manifests an *inclusio* in that it starts and ends with the verb qrʾ. In the first relative clause (ᵃšær jiqraʾ) the faithful people of Yahweh are the subject, and Yahweh himself is the subject of the second relative clause. Hence in a sense there is a correlation between the qrʾ of the people and the qrʾ of Yahweh.

The content of this pericope section refers back to and elaborates on the credal formula in 2 27. At the same time it forms a transition to the judgment of the enemy nations in the next chapter.[11]

Unlike the previous two strophes, 5 abc is not a speech by Yahweh but speaks about him. It follows that 1b–2 and 3–4b should link primarily with one another (1a serves to introduce both strophes), whereupon 5 abc connects with the preceding part as a sort of prophetic comment. But even in this final strophe the "prophetic comment" is based on a saying of Yahweh.

It should be noted that this pericope repeats words and phrases mainly from 2 1–11, and especially the Yom Yahweh terminology (cf. 3 4b with 2 11c; 3 4a with 2 10a and b). The wᵉgăm-pᵉlêṭā loʾ-hajᵉtā (2 3c) contrasts strikingly with kî bᵉhăr-ṣijjon … tihᵉjæh pᵉlêṭā, indicating that judgment has changed to blessing and that there is still hope of redemption.

The *metre* does not help much to explain the structure. Keller[12] observes: "le rythme est assez irréguliér . . .", which has led exegetes to arrive at widely differing conclusions about it.[13]

---

[10] One therefore has to agree with Rudolph, KAT XIII/2, 70/71.
[11] Cf. Deden, op. cit., 107.
[12] Op. cit., 140; Wolff, BKAT XIV/2, 70.
[13] Cf. e.g. Allen, op. cit., 96/97; Bewer, op. cit., 121/122; Robinson op. cit., 65 and 67.

By and large the *Gáttung* of this pericope could be called a *promise of salvation*.[14] In the first two strophes it takes the form of a speech by Yahweh, characterized by his speaking in the first person singular and addressing the people in the second person plural. In the final strophe (3 5) Yahweh is no longer speaking personally; this could perhaps best be described as an eschatological *Lehrsatz*.[15]

It is impossible to determine the cultic or historical *Sitz im Leben* of the pericope exactly. At most one can argue, as the analysis indicates, that it has a meaningful place in the present literary *Sitz*.

Various traditions and other conventional material are used in this passage, but one could say that the author uses these distinctively for his own purposes. The *Yom Yahweh tradition* features once more in terminology manifestly relating to that of 2 1—11 (cf. 3 4b with 2 11 c and 3 4a with 2 10a and b). In 3 4b the jôm is described as hăggadôl wᵉhănnorā', but in strophe 3 3—4b it is mainly a matter of the môpᵉtîm which precede the jôm (lipnê-4b). Hence the môpᵉtîm are indeed portents of the Yom Yahweh. The context of 2—4b and the way the môpᵉtîm are described shed light on the function and meaning of the Yom Yahweh tradition in this pericope.

When we were considering the *Gattung* the pericope was defined as a promise of salvation: 1b—2 is indeed Yahweh's act of mercy to his whole people, and 5 abc a promise that he offers deliverance and salvation. The preceding pericope (2 18—27) likewise deals with Yahweh's promise of salvation to his people, and the next one (4 1ff.) with the judgment on foreign nations. From the context it is clearly a case of *salvation* for Israel and *judgment* on the nations, and this is the framework in which one should see both the portents and the jôm itself. The jôm no longer bodes ill for Israel, only for the nations. Clearly the Yom Yahweh tradition is not used in the same way here as in 2 1—11, where the day was to be one of doom — for Yahweh's people as well. In the present pericope it functions ambivalently, bringing salvation for Israel and doom for the nations. This is also evident from the way in which the portents of the jôm are described. There is no doubt that Joel is using conventional material to depict the Yom Yahweh: môpᵉtîm (3) is a conventional term from the *exodus tradition*, used in conjunction with 'ot and nipla'ôt[16] to describe Yahweh's wondrous deeds dur-

---

14 Although Wolff regards the whole of 2 19—27 and 3 1—5 as an *Erhörungswort*, he acknowledges that the *specific* characteristics of this *Gattung* are not to be found in 3 1—5 (cf. BKAT XIV/2, 69).

15 H.-P. Müller, op. cit., 243.

16 Robinson, op. cit., 66 differentiates the three terms as follows: "אוֹת ist ein 'Zeichen', das kein Wunder zu sein braucht; פֶּלֶא ist ein Wunder, das keine besondere Bedeutung zu haben

ing the exodus from Egypt.[17] By using this familiar term from the ancient tradition Yahweh's act of deliverance towards his people is portrayed as a type of new exodus. The môpᵉtîm is also described conventionally as dam waʾeš wᵉtimᵃrôt ʿašan (3) blood, fire and columns of smoke are images normally associated with *war*.[18] Other môpᵉtîm is the cosmic upheaval (4a: haššæmæš jehapek lᵉḥôšæk wᵉhăjjareaḥ lᵉdam) which will darken the sun and turn the moon to blood. Clearly the author of Joel is once again using traditional terms, for cosmic changes are often associated with Yahweh's punishments and rebukes.[19] Thus the portents characterize the jôm as a day of terror, so that in this respect Joel 3 is no different to 2 1—11. Rudolph[20] isolates the new element in Joel 3: "Israel bleibt die Angst vor diesen Phänomenen erspart." The fire, blood and columns of fire on earth and cosmic changes in the heavens therefore signify that doomsday has changed to a day of salvation. The way in which Yahweh's intervention is portrayed raises the question whether in Joel we have an early instance of apocalyptic literature. G. von Rad expresses a word of caution in this regard:[21] "Wer den Begriff Apokalyptik verwendet, sollte sich der Tatsache bewußt bleiben, daß es bisher noch nicht gelungen ist, ihn auf eine befriedigende Weise zu definieren . . ." There is absolutely no consensus on the relation between eschatology and apocalyptic. Quite often scholars use terminology deriving from our Western thought system and project it onto the Old Testament.[22]

The exact meaning of apocalyptic[23] and its essential features and origins[24] are, in the nature of things, much disputed. Hence it would appear to

---

braucht; מוֹפֵת ist beides: ein Wunder, das zugleich ein Zeichen ist und denen, die weise genug sind, es zu verstehen, eine göttliche Botschaft vermittelt." Cf. also Wolff, BKAT XIV/2, 81 and M. Bič, op. cit., 83.

[17] Cf. Ex 7 13; Dtn 6 22; I Chr 16 12; Neh 9 10; Jer 32 20; Ps 78 43; 105 5, 27; 136 9.
[18] Cf. e.g. Num 21 28; Jos 8 18ff.; Jdc 20 38ff.; Ps 78 63.
[19] Cf. Am 8 9; Isa 13 10; Ez 32 7; cf. Zeph 1 14ff. where it is also used in relation to the Yom Yahweh. It is illuminating that in both Isa 13 16 and Ez 32 7 the cosmic disturbances are associated with judgments on foreign nations — in Isa 13 on Babylon and in Ez 32 on Egypt. In this respect Joel therefore concurs with Ezekiel and Isaiah.
[20] KAT XIII/2, 73.
[21] Theologie des Alten Testaments Band II, ⁵1968, 316.
[22] Cf. Th. C. Vriezen, Prophecy and Eschatology, SVT1 (1953), 200.
[23] For an introduction to the problems of apocalyptic literature, cf. M. A. Beek, Inleiding in de Joodse Apokalyptiek van het Oud- en Nieuw-Testamentisch Tijdvak (Theologia VI), 1950; S. B. Frost, Old Testament Apocalyptic, 1952; G. von Rad, Theologie des AT II, 1968, 316ff.; O. Plöger, Theokratie und Eschatologie, 1959, 37—68; J. M. Schmidt, Die jüdische Apokalyptik, 1969; I. Willi-Plein, Das Geheimnis der Apokalyptik, VT 22 (1977), 62—81; P. D. Hanson, The dawn of Apocalyptic, 1975, offers a sociological explanation of

be quite impossible to determine whether or not the book of Joel — or parts of it — is apocalyptic literature.[25]

From this pericope however one can infer that the outpouring of Yahweh's rûăḥ and the accompanying cosmic upheavals usher in a new age of salvation for Israel. The cosmic changes are portrayed in hyperboles to stress their radical nature. Depending on one's definition of eschatology and apocalyptic one could classify this pericope under either one or the other!

Finally we should also mention the *Zion tradition*. In 5b, the substantiation of 5a, it is explicitly stated that there is deliverance in Zion and in

---

the dawn of apocalyptic. Cf. also F. E. Deist, Prior to the dawn of apocalyptic, OTWSA 25 (1982)/OTWSA 26 (1983), 13—38 who seeks to broaden the basis of Hanson's theory.

[24] G. von Rad, Theologie des AT II, 1968, 316 believes that the origins of O. T. apocalyptic should be traced to wisdom literature. Peter von der Osten-Sacken, Die Apokalyptik in ihrem Verhältnis zu Prophetie und Weisheit (Theologische Existenz Heute nr 157), 1969, 9—62 rejects Von Rad's thesis that apocalyptic is an offshoot of wisdom, but sees it rather as a "legitimes wenn auch eigenartige Kind der Prophetie" (63). Apocalyptic is based on later prophecy, specifically that of Deutero-Isaiah where history is made subject to divine predestination. H. Gese, Anfang und Ende der Apokalyptik dargestellt am Sacharjabuch, ZThK 70 (1973), 20—49 claims that *formally* Ezekiel is a precursor of apocalyptic, whereas Deutero-Isaiah prefigures its *content*. In Deutero-Isaiah Yahweh's coming is the goal and end of history and his royal sovereignty constitutes the eventual apocalyptic. However Gese sees Zechariah's visions as the "älteste uns bekannte Apokalypse." (24). G. Edwards, The Exodus and Apocalyptic (in A Stubborn Faith-Presented to W. A. Irwin), 1956, 27—38 traces the origin of apocalyptic to the exodus tradition which it reinterprets: "The point of transition from prophecy to apocalyptic therefore is to be found in the sixth century B. C." (36). O. Plöger, op. cit., 37—68, sees prophetic eschatology as the basis of apocalyptic. Eschatology was evolved into apocalyptic by a group outside the priestly aristocracy. Willi-Plein, VT 27 (1977), 62—81 finds the "Wesensbestimmung" of apocalyptic in Daniel, maintaining that, by contrast with prophecy, apocalyptic is marked by (i) pseudonymity; (ii) the fact that its author is no prophet but his work is *angelus interpretes*; and (iii) mystery, whereas prophecy is revelation. M. Noth, Das Geschichtsverständnis der alttestamentlichen Apokalyptik (Theologische Bücherei 6), ³1966, 250 also sees Daniel as the source of O. T. apocalyptic. For a recent characterization of apocalyptic, cf. O. H. Steck, Überlegungen zur Eigenart der spätisraelitischen Apokalyptik (Die Botschaft und die Boten, Festschrift für H. W. Wolff) 1981, 301—315. Steck firmly believes that Joel should not be regarded as apocalyptic (personal communication).

[25] Wolff, BKAT XIV/2, 13 plays it safe by saying that Joel is on the brink of "prophetischen zur apokalyptischen Eschatologie". Th. C. Vriezen, op. cit., 219 maintains that Joel reaches the borderline of later apocalyptics. M. A. Beek, op. cit., 18 claims that if one can at all speak of apocalyptic with reference to Joel it would apply only to the formal aspects. Ahlström, op. cit., 91 writes: "... Joel is not an apocalyptic book ... Joel may have contributed to the beginning of apocalyptic — or, he may even have inspired that beginning ...". No matter how cautiously they are formulated, each of these statements is based on a particular view of what is meant by apocalyptic.

Jerusalem. This is a classical use of the tradition. Zion and Jerusalem are pre-eminently the abode of Yahweh, citadels of security and stability. Thus in saying that there is deliverance in Zion and in Jerusalem, the author is referring to the deliverance offered by Yahweh himself. In the midst of calamity and cosmic upheaval Yahweh is the one who offers his people security.

The *redaction history* of 3 1–5 relates to that of the book as a whole. Firstly one must consider the relation of 3 1–5 to the rest of the book. Duhm's view, that 2 18–4 21 is an *Ergänzerarbeit* written in prose, is widely known:[26] Duhm maintained that 2 18–27 was the introduction and that the apocalyptic editor only got round to eschatology proper in 3 1–5. Duhm's view of the redaction history of Joel was widely influential, and he was followed to a greater or lesser extent by such scholars as H. Birkeland,[27] J. A. Bewer,[28] E. Sellin[29] and T. H. Robinson.[30]

Exponents of the unity of Joel,[31] however, reacted strongly against Duhm's thesis. Among modern scholars O. Plöger is one of the few who do not accept the unity of the book. His view of the redaction history of Joel, and particularly of chapter 3,[32] is fascinating: Chapters 1 and 2 are said to be a written record of Joel's oral message. The locust plague was amplified and reinterpreted by means of traditional material of the Yom Yahweh, thereby giving the locusts eschatological overtones. The addition of chapter 4 effects a "Re-Eschatologisierung" of chapters 1 and 2. The "Einschaltung" (integration) of chapter 3 came after this. Compared with chapters 1, 2 and 4, chapter 3 is *sui generis*. Its function is to indicate that the promises in chapter 4 are true, but at the same time to impose a sort of limit: "Noch wird ganz Israel die Rettung am Tage Jahwes zugesprochen, aber es kann sich dabei nur um jenes Israel handeln, das sich dem eschatologischen Glauben geöffnet hat und mit dem Tage Jahwes als mit einer eschatologischen Größe rechnet."[33]

---

[26] Cf. Duhm, ZAW 31 (1911), 187.
[27] Zum hebräischen Traditionswesen. Die Komposition der prophetischen Bücher des Alten Testaments, 1938, 64–66.
[28] Cf. op. cit.
[29] Cf. op. cit.
[30] Cf. op. cit.
[31] Cf. W. S. Prinsloo, Die boek Joël: Verleentheid of geleentheid?, NGTT XXIV (1983), 256ff.
[32] O. Plöger, op. cit., 117–128.
[33] O. Plöger, op. cit., 125.

Intriguing as Plöger's hypothesis may be, one has to concede B. S. Child's[34] point about it: "It is obvious that Plöger's theory assumes a very complex literary development behind the present form of the book. Even if such a growth could be shown, it remains a very speculative enterprise to reconstruct an unknown period of Israel's postexilic history on the basis of literary tensions within a text which seem to have been both set up and resolved in order to confirm the historical thesis." The current trend, namely adherence to the unity of Joel, is plausibly substantiated.[35] The credit for demonstrating this unity and identifying the symmetrical structure of the book belongs to Wolff.[36]

It is all but impossible, however, to determine whether this unity is indicative of a single author[37] or of a redactor who deliberately contrived it.[38] The important point is the book as we have it today. Our analysis so far has shown that Joel constitutes a meaningful whole and should be interpreted as such. As regards the relation of 3 1–5 to the rest, on the one hand it links up neatly with the preceding part (weʰajah ʾăḥªrê-ken), on the other it provides a logical transition to the next pericope (4 1 ff. –judgment on the nations).

We should not limit ourselves to the redaction history of 3 1–5 as an entity, but should also consider the various elements of the pericope. Robinson[39] believes that a later redactor inserted the weʰajah ʾăḥªrê-ken so as to effect a link with the preceding passage. He argues that there is no *waw* consecutive before ʾæšpôk (1b), whereas weʰajah is usually followed by such a consecutive. H.-P. Müller,[40] however, explodes Robinson's argument by pointing out that Sach 14 7b, 8 shows that weʰajah can also be followed by an imperfect. Bič[41] exposes another flaw in Robinson's logic by indicating that the alleged redactor would have had no difficulty in adding the waw as well.

Robinson[42] is equally convinced that 3 2 – which he regards as a prosaic "Weiterausmalung" of verse 1 – is secondary. Deden[43] agrees, citing as

[34] Introduction to the Old Testament as Scripture, 1979, 388. Cf. also H.-P. Müller, Theologia Viatorum 10 (1965/6), 248, footnote 52.

[35] Cf. W. S. Prinsloo, NGTT XXIV (1983), 256 ff.

[36] BKAT XIV/2, especially 5 ff.

[37] Wolff, BKAT XIV/2, 7: "... man zerstört von vornherein die Verständnismöglichkeit, wenn man sie zwei verschiedenen Verfassern zuweist."

[38] Childs, Introduction, 389: "I tend to think that the unity is redactional."

[39] Op. cit., 65–66. Cf. also Bewer, op. cit., 122.

[40] Op. cit., 241–242.   [41] Op. cit., 80.

[42] Robinson, op. cit., 66; cf. also Sellin, op. cit., 170.

[43] Deden, op. cit., 106–107.

further grounds the presence of găm, băjjamim hahemmā in 2, where the
start of 1b ('æšpôk 'æt-rûhî) is repeated. Rudolph[44] refutes these arguments: "Das bedeutet nicht, daß es sich um einen späteren Zusatz handelt.
. . . Die Wiederholung der Zeitbestimmung und des Wortlautes . . . bezeugt
nur, wie sehr sich Joel der Bedeutsamkeit seiner Aussage bewußt war. . . ."

Our analysis[45] confirms this: 1b—2 displays a clear *inclusio*, accompanied moreover by a chiastic structure. The w^egăm is deliberately placed in
a prominent position at the beginning of stich 2, further elaborating on the
preceding stichs. It would be a flagrant contradiction of the whole structure
— both formal and as regards content — of 1b—2 to regard 2 as a later addition.

Robinson[46] takes his argument further by averring that 3 3—5 is an
apocalyptic fragment, which was amplified in prose (i. e. 3 5) prior to its
inclusion in Joel.

O. Plöger conclusively demonstrated the unity of 3 1—5,[47] and our
structural analysis revealed an *inclusio* in 5a—c. This is an additional argument in favour of the unity of the passage.[48]

After this synchronic and diachronic study we can now arrive at a
meaningful synthesis of the *theology* of the pericope. Although it is closely
linked to the previous one, it heralds a new era of salvation for Yahweh's
people.

Strophe 1b—2 deals with the outpouring of Yahweh's spirit ('æšpôk
'æt-rûhî). The *inclusio* greatly accentuates Yahweh's acts: he takes the initiative; the outpouring of his rûăh governs all further events.[49] Just as he revi-
talized nature by "pouring out" his rain (cf. 2 24), so he gives his people
new life by the outpouring of his rûăh. It is not so much a case of a new

---

[44] Rudolph, KAT XIII/2, 72—73.

[45] Cf. discussion above.

[46] Robinson, op. cit., 67. Jepsen, ZAW 56 (1932), 86—87, partly concurs with this, regarding
3 4—5 as an apocalyptic addition. Rudolph, KAT XIII/2, 70 footnote 5 sees the last four
words of 3 5c as another later addition.

[47] Cf. op. cit., 124 for his arguments.

[48] The only possible redactional addition is the latter part of 5b (cf. Wolff, BKAT XIV/2, 81)
its function being to make it quite clear that the prophetic "comment" in 5 abc is also based
on Yahweh's own words. The first part of 5b, kî b^ehăr-şijjôn ûbîrûšalăim tih^ejæh p^elêţā,
closely resembles Ob 17. Whether Obadiah depends on Joel or vice versa is hard to say.
Most exegetes' views are governed by their dating of the book (cf. the commentaries and
relevant literature).

[49] Joel is "quoted" and reinterpreted in Acts 2. For this, cf. A. Kerrigan, The "sensus plenior"
of Joel III, 1—5, in Act., II, 14—36 (Sacra Pagina II, — Bibliotheca Ephermeridum Theologicarum Lovaniensum 12/13, 1959), 295—315.

morality for Israel or a large-scale conversion of gentile nations.[50] The context clearly indicates that this is divine vitality given to kål-baśar which finds expression in prophecies, visions and dreams. The specification of kål-baśar in 1b and c makes it clear that the reference is to Israel. Yahweh gives his rûăḥ to his people irrespective of sex, age or social status. The "charismatic gifts" are not reserved for some select soul such as a prophet or a king: the whole nation consists of fully authorized agencies of revelation.[51] Thus the outpouring of Yahweh's rûăḥ attests to a new relation between him and his people and is a closer specification of the kî beqæræb jiśra'el 'anî in 2 27a.

Yahweh's act of salvation is further emphasized by the first person singular natǎtti and the passive jehapek (4a). It is Yahweh who effects the môpetîm, which are more closely defined in 3/4b as portents of the Yom Yahweh. From the context it is evident that, by contrast with 2 1—11, the Yom does not bode peril and doom for Yahweh's people, but that it will be a day of salvation. Hence the môpetîm is a sign of a special act of salvation by Yahweh — a new exodus as it were.

The môpetîm is described in conventional terms usually associated with the wrath of Yahweh. Here it spells salvation for Israel who is spared the terrors of the Yom. The hyperbolical account of the portents which affect the entire cosmos (heaven and earth) stress the radical nature both of the new era of salvation and of Yahweh's act.[52]

The prophetic comment in 5 abc — which links up with 2 27 but also with the next pericope — adds a new dimension to the promised new era of salvation: the Zion tradition is invoked to stress that Yahweh offers security and stability. But the promise of salvation is not unqualified. There is a correlation between the qr' of Yahweh and that of the people — the 'aśærjiqra' bešem jhwh does not denote mere lip service, but assumes that man will believe in Yahweh, trust in him and confess him in word and deed.[53]

---

[50] Contra D. Lys, "Ruach" le souffle dans l'Ancien Testament, 1962, 247—248.

[51] Cf. Num 11 29, Moses' prayer: "Would that all the Lord's people were prophets, that the Lord would put his spirit upon them."

[52] Cf. A. Weiser, op. cit., 120 who writes as follows: "Das Wesentliche des Glaubens an diesen Zukunftsvorstellungen ... ist die Perspektive, daß Gott selbst die letzten Dinge nach seinem Willen gestaltet und seine Herrschaft darin sichert, daß er die Menschen unmittelbar an sich bindet und für diese Lebensbeziehung fähig macht."

[53] Deden, op. cit., 107.

(1) 4 1–8

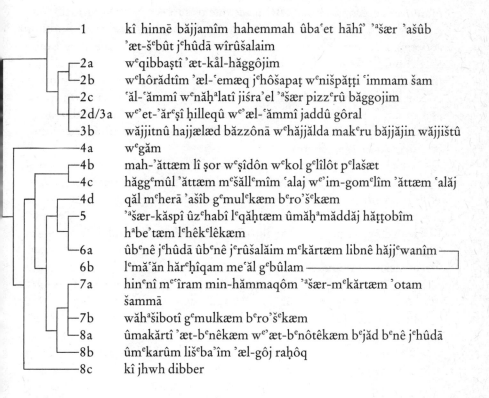

1   kî hinnē bǎjjamîm hahemmah ûbaʿet hāhî ʾᵃšær ʾašûb
    ʾæt-šᵉbût jᵉhûdā wîrûšalaim

2a   wᵉqibbaṣtî ʾæt-kål-hǎggôjim

2b   wᵉhôrădtîm ʾæl-ʿemæq jᵉhôšapaṭ wᵉnišpǎṭṭi ʿimmam šam

2c   ʿål-ʿǎmmî wᵉnǎḥᵃlatî jiśraʾel ʾᵃšær pizzᵉrû bǎggojim

2d/3a wᵉʾet-ʾǎrᵉṣî ḥilleqû wᵉʾæl-ʿǎmmî jaddû gôral

3b   wǎjjitnû hajjælæd bǎzzônā wᵉhǎjjǎlda makᵉru bǎjjǎjin wǎjjištû

4a   wᵉgǎm

4b   mah-ʾåttæm lî ṣor wᵉṣîdôn wᵉkol gᵉlîlôt pᵉlašæt

4c   hǎggᵉmûl ʾåttæm mᵉšållᵉmîm ʿalaj wᵉʾim-gomᵉlîm ʾåttæm ʿalǎj

4d   qǎl mᵉherā ʾašîb gᵉmulᵉkæm bᵉroʾšᵉkæm

5   ʾᵃšær-kǎspî ûzᵉhabî lᵉqǎḥtæm ûmǎḥᵃmăddǎj hǎṭṭobîm
    hᵃbeʾtæm lᵉhêkᵉlêkæm

6a   ûbᵉnê jᵉhûdā ûbᵉnê jᵉrûšalǎim mᵉkǎrtæm libnê hǎjjᵉwanîm

6b   lᵉmǎʿan hǎrᵉḥîqam meʿål gᵉbûlam

7a   hinᵉnî mᵉʿîram min-hǎmmaqôm ʾᵃšær-mᵉkǎrtæm ʾotam
    šammā

7b   wǎhᵃšibotî gᵉmulkæm bᵉroʾšᵉkæm

8a   ûmakǎrtî ʾæt-bᵉnêkæm wᵉʾæt-bᵉnôtêkæm bᵉjǎd bᵉnê jᵉhûdā

8b   ûmᵉkarûm lišᵉbaʾîm ʾæl-gôj raḥôq

8c   kî jhwh dibber

    This fourth chapter of Joel has probably stirred up more scholarly debate than any other chapter of the book, particularly as regards dating it.

    Since the chapter is said to contain ''historical'' references it is fairly widely used for purposes of dating the book. But when one compares the different attempts one is amazed to find that one and the same text is often

---

[1] The poetic classification of BHS is our premise for stichs 4a–8c.

used to arrive at totally divergent findings.[2] Often a preconceived notion of
the date has a profound impact on the exegesis, resulting in a subjective
slant on the whole book. Sometimes the text is "twisted" to fit an exegete's
proposed dating. Such preconceptions – particularly methodological ones
– often play a far greater role in the dating of the book than most scholars
will concede.

Dating is and will always be important. After all, a historical framework provides an extremely useful instrument for understanding a text. But
the mere fact that attempted datings of the book of Joel range from the
ninth to the second century BC leads one to suspect that it is virtually impossible to date it exactly purely on the basis of its contents. Without
adopting an ahistorical approach or ignoring the problems, the sincere exegete should acknowledge this fact. And if it is conceded that it is all but
impossible to date the book satisfactorily, he must adopt the only other
course left to him, namely to use the text of Joel itself to the utmost to try
and discover its actual message and intention. Since the historical context
cannot be accurately reconstructed, the book has to be expounded within
its intrinsic literary context.

Chapter 4 1–17 represents a *demarcated pericope* introduced by a conventional formula, kî hinne băjjamîm hahemmah.[3] This pericope is however linked with the preceding one by means of "ein begründendes כִּי".[4] As a
result the promised deliverance in Jerusalem and on Mount Zion is amplified by Yahweh's judgment on the nations.[5] At the other end the pericope is
demarcated by the introductory formula wᵉhajah băjjôm hăhû' in 4 18a.
Thematically it is unified in its concentration on Yahweh's judgment on the
nations. There are also lexeme and phrase recurrences:[6] gôjim (2a, 2c, 9a,
12a, 12b); the verb stems ʿûr (7a, 9b, 12a); qbṣ (2a, 11a); mkr (3b, 6a, 7a,
8a, 8b); špṭ (2b, 12b); the phrase 'æl-ʿemæq jᵉhôšapaṭ (2b, 12a); and in variant form bᵉʿemæq hæḥarûṣ (14a, 14b).

The pericope is composed of several *sections* which will emerge clearly
when we come to discuss its overall structure.

---

[2] Cf. W. S. Prinsloo, Die boek Joël: verleentheid of geleentheid?, NGTT XXIV (1983),
258ff. for a survey of the various attempts at dating the book.

[3] Cf. Jer 50 4, 20; 33 15.

[4] Cf. H.-P. Müller, Theologia Viatorum 10 (1965/66), 243.

[5] Wolff, BKAT XIV/2, 88; H.-M. Lutz, Jahwe, Jerusalem und die Völker, 54.

[6] We shall deal with the repetition of lexemes and phrases within a single pericope ad loc.

Next we must turn to the main *text-critical problems*. The *hapax legomenon* ʿûšû (11a) has prompted various proposals to improve the text,[7] but
a *hapax legomenon* does not constitute adequate grounds for textual emendation. The context suggests that ʿûšû is an imperative relating to the summons to war.[8]

The form niqbaṣû (11a) (Nifal perfect, third person plural) also strikes
one as peculiar. One would have expected another imperative in keeping
with the preceding ones. This problem too has led to various possible solutions.[9] The context leaves one no choice but to read an imperative in this
case as well. It is moreover logical to link (11a) with šamma, even though it
conflicts with the accentuation.[10]

Line 11b as a whole (hănᵉḥăt jhwh gibbôrᵃ̈ka) also poses a text-critical
problem. The completely deviant reading of the LXX[11] indicates that this

---

[7] LXX, Targum and the Syriac version render it with something like "assemble"; on the
strength of 9b and 12b the change to ʿûrû has considerable support: cf. K. Marti, Das Dodekapropheton, 1904, 140; W. Nowack, Die Kleinen Propheten, ³1922, 107; Sellin, op. cit.,
175; H.-M. Lutz, op. cit., 56; Robinson, op. cit., 68 wants to read חושו ("hurry") – cf.
also BHK³ ad loc.

[8] Cf. Rudolph, KAT XIII/2, 77 and Rudolph, SVT 16 (1967), 249 for an Arabic verb ġawiṭ
("run fast") and an Arabic adverb ġašašan ("fast", "quickly") which may act as a compara-
tive.

[9] niqbaṣû is sometimes regarded as an irregular form of the imperative (cf. Allen, op. cit.
107); M. Dahood, Hebrew-Ugaritic Lexicography IX, Biblica 52 (1971), 342 writes: "In
Joel 4, 11, the balance with two imperatives underlines the precative character of niqbāṣû."
Several scholars are in favour of changing the text to hiqqabᵉṣû (Nif. Imper.) (cf. Robinson,
op. cit., 68; Wolff, BKAT XIV/2, 87; Sellin, op. cit., 175; Lutz, op. cit., 56; BHS, ad loc.).
Rudolph KAT XIII/2, 77, following O. Procksch, Die kleinen prophetischen Schriften
nach dem Exil, 1916, 87 tries to solve the problem by completely inverting the text, trans-
posing the last five words of 11 to the end of 12. Rudolph's hypothesis is that these words
were omitted as a result of a copying error and were then reinstated mistakenly after the
first kâl-hăggôjim missabîb (11a) instead of after the second, kâl hăggôjim missabîb (12b).
This change would solve the problem, permitting a rendering of, "Sind sie aber dort ver-
sammelt, so laß, Jahwe, deine Mächtigen herabfahren!" Rudolph's is an attractive hypothesis, but one would need more textual evidence to justify such a radical inversion.

[10] Cf. Lutz, op. cit., 56.

[11] LXX's ὁ πραὺς ἔστω μαχητής means something like "The meek will be a hero". This rendering has considerable support: cf. e.g. Bewer op. cit., 139; Robinson, op. cit., 68; Sellin,
op. cit., 175; Allen, op. cit., 107, wants to read "hanniḥăṭ yehî gibbôr" ("Let the timid man
become a hero") which amounts to the same as the LXX reading. The Targum, Syriac version, Vulgate leave the Massoretic text as it is, linking hănᵉḥăt with ḥtt (cf. Kapelrud, op.
cit., 161). Wolff, BKAT XIV/2, 87–88 and Lutz, op. cit., 56, agree, reading wăjjiḥăt jhwh
gibbôrᵃ̈ka ("... daß Jahwe deine Helden zerschmettere"). Wolff apparently follows the
principle that (88) "... im Kontext ist eine Anrede Jahwes höchst unwahrscheinlich".
Hence in his view the gibbôrᵃ̈ka refers to the armies not of Yahweh but of the enemy.

stich presented a *crux interpretum* from the outset. The simplest solution
would be to leave the Massoretic reading untouched and to interpret hăn^e-
ḥăt as a hifil imperative, of nḥt[12] rendering it with, "Let your heroes come
down, o Yahweh".

Having established the best reading of the text, we must turn to the
structure of the pericope. Yahweh's action is expressed climactically by
means of three first person singular verbs: qibbaṣtî (2a), hôrădtîm (2b) and
nišpaṭṭî. nišpaṭṭî must be interpreted as a *nifil tolerativum*[13] indicating Yahweh as the prosecutor instituting legal action against the gôjim. špṭ can in
fact be seen as *Stichwort*.[14] The syntactic link between 2a and 2b is rein-
forced by the recurrence of the object (gôjim) in 2b via the third person
plural pronominal suffixes (w^ehôrădtîm, ʿimmam).

Lines 2c, 3a and 3b together state the reason for the lawsuit. This is
achieved by the prominent position of ʿăl (2c) in the syntax. It is amplified
by a relative clause specifying the action of the gôjim. The culpable act of
the gôjim is powerfully stressed by a cumulation of no fewer than six verbs
in the third person plural: pizz^erû (2c), hilleqû, jaddû (3a), wăjjitnû, mak^e-
ru, wăjjištû (3b).

The first person singular suffix at ʿămmî, năḥ^alatî (2c), ʾăr^eṣî, ʿămmî
(3a) is striking, stressing that the crime was against Yahweh's "property".

2c/3a b connects with the preceding 2a b in that – as pointed out already – 2c/3a b states the reason for Yahweh's legal action. The combination 2abc/ 3ab as a whole connects with 1. Yahweh is the subject in both 1
and 2a, and 2a–3b explains in negative terms what the ʾašûb ʾæt-š^ebût will
comprise.

The next pericope section starts at 4a. Most scholars regard 4a–8c as a
later editorial addition[15] but the point is not relevant here. Because of our
synchronic approach we must first see how this passage fits into the structure and content of the pericope. Firstly one observes that the mak^eru of 3b
is repeated and elevated to a *Leitwort* (m^ekărtæm-6a, 7a; makărtî-8a; m^eka-
rûm-8b). Yahweh's speech with its first person singular verb and suffixes is
continued, as are the third person plural suffixes referring to the object. The

---

Kapelrud, op. cit., 161, claims, and one must concede his point, that there is no really
cogent reason why the stich should not be seen as a prayer to Yahweh.
[12] Rudolph, KAT XIII/2, 77 points out that this Aramaic equivalent of jrd also occurs in Jer
21 13. Cf. also Kapelrud, op. cit., 162; M. Bič, op. cit., 96 and P. D. Miller, The divine
council and the prophetic call to war, VT 18 (1968), 103–104.
[13] Wolff, BKAT XIV/2, 92; Deden, op. cit., 109.
[14] Cf. also 12b and the manifest word-play here in 2b and in 12a (j^ehôšapaṭ).
[15] Cf. detailed discussion below.

word play introduced in 4 1 (ʾašûb ʾæt-sᵉbût) is continued (ʾašîb-4d). The lawsuit of 4 1−3 actually opens in 4 4−8 with the rhetorical questions. The wᵉgăm introducing 4a patently refers back to the preceding verses, but also takes them to a climax. Verses 4 4−8 are clearly a closer definition and concretization of the gôjim referred to generally in 4 1−3: here they are mentioned by name.

Thus 4 4−8 links up quite well with what goes before. The section is structured as follows: 4b and 4c are linked due to the interrogative particles introducing both lines (mah-4b; ha-4c). The personal pronoun ʾăttæm is also a striking feature of both, as is the first person suffix to the prepositions (lî-4b; ʿalaj-4c). The second half line of 4c (wᵉʾim . . .) is best read as another rhetorical question rather than a conditional clause. Poetic parallelism would indicate two rhetorical questions.[16] These questions, both presupposing a negative answer, establish the guilt of the accused beyond all doubt and lead to the "threats" in the ensuing lines.

Verse 5, a relative clause introduced by ᵃʾšær, clearly links up with the preceding lines. Although the ᵃʾšær is not repeated, the relative clause is continued in 6a. Stichs 6a and 5 moreover share the same subject − the nations − as indicated by the second person plural verbs (lᵉqăḥtæm-5; hᵃbeʾtæm-5; mᵉkărtæm-6a). Note also the conspicuous *waw* copulative at the start of 6a. The combination 5, 6a thus links up with 4d. Stich 6b, by means of lᵉmăʿan, reflects the consequence of the mᵉkărtæm in 6a. The object, (bᵉnê jᵉhûdā ûbᵉnê jᵉrûšalăim-6a) is repeated in 6b by means of third person plural suffixes (hărᵉḥîqam, gᵉbûlam), thus linking up specifically with 6a.

The words qăl and mᵉhera (4d) together form a superlative,[17] stressing the speed of Yahweh's action. Through the listing of the doings of the gôjîm, 5 and 6a substantiate Yahweh's punitive action. The mounting list of verbs accentuate the atrocities committed by the nations. The first person singular suffixes in 5 (kăspî, zᵉhabî, măḥᵃmăddăj) stress Yahweh's sovereign ownership of the treasures of the land. By robbing these the nations have therefore transgressed against Yahweh himself.

7a, b, 8a, b are linked serially by means of the succession of *waw* copulatives. Syntactically 7a, b and 8a are more closey connected in that Yahweh is the subject of the action. On the *positive* side this action is that he will deliver his people from slavery. hinᵉnî (7a) focuses attention on his intervention. Being followed by a participle, it refers to the imminent future.[18]

---

[16] Allen, op. cit., 106. Cf. also Joel 1 2.
[17] Deden, op. cit., 109.
[18] Allen, op. cit., 111.

On the *negative* side Yahweh's action consists in visiting upon the nations their transgressions (7b). This is specified more closely in 8a and b.

For various reasons the combination 7a–8b links up with the preceding 4a–6b. As in the preceding stich section, Yahweh is again the subject in 7a–8b; stich 7b repeats part of 4d almost verbatim (wăhᵃšibotî gᵉ-mulkæm). Stich 7a–8b reiterates mkr from 6a, elevating it to a *Leitwort* (7a, 8a, 8b); at 7a the object in 6b (hărᵉḥîqam) is repeated via a third person suffix mᵉᶜîram. In 8b the stem rḥq is deliberately used (raḥôq) for the sake of a contrast with 6b (hărᵉḥîqam).

If one studies the combination 4a–8b in its entirety the following picture emerges. The roles have been completely reversed:

$$
\left\{
\begin{array}{l}
\text{6a: } ûbᵉnê\ jᵉhûdā\ \dots\ mᵉkărtæm \\
\qquad \textit{has changed to} \\[1em]
\text{8a: } ûmᵉkărtî\ ’æt\ \dots\dots\ bᵉjăd\ bᵉnê\ jᵉhûdā \\
\qquad\qquad\qquad\qquad\quad \textit{and}
\end{array}
\right.
$$

$$
\left\{
\begin{array}{l}
\text{6b: } lᵉmăᶜan\ hărᵉḥîqam \\
\qquad \textit{has changed to} \\[1em]
\text{8b: } ’æl - gôj\ raḥôq
\end{array}
\right.
$$

The repetition of the refrain (4d, 7b) makes it clear that the changed situation is Yahweh's doing.

Stichs 4bc logically connect with 4d–8b; in both sections Yahweh is the speaker addressing the nations.

8c is overarchingly linked with the preceding speech by Yahweh (4b–8b). The function of the kî is probably affirmative, so that stich 8c confirms yet again that the preceding was Yahweh's own authoritive words. Obviously wᵉgăm (4a) connects overarchingly with the rest of the pericope section.

There is no consensus about the *metre* of 4 4–8. BHK³ prints this passage as prose, BHS as verse. Most commentators are inclined to see this passage as prose, or to describe its style as prosaic.[19] A few scholars regard it as poetry, for instance J. A. Thompson who writes: "These verses are also rhythmic. The long measures are suitable to a solemn indictment".[20] A

---

[19] Cf. the commentaries ad loc.
[20] IB 6, 755. Cf also Allen, op. cit., 106.

final judgment is virtually impossible, but since one has to decide one way or the other, we shall settle for the poetic subdivision of the BHS.

The next pericope section, commencing at 4 9, is set apart from 4 4—8 by a striking series of imperatives. The structure of this section is as follows:

(2) 4 9—17

9a	qirʾû-zoʾt băggôjim qăddᵉšû milḥamā
9b	haʿîrû hăggibbôrîm jiggᵉšû jăʿᵃlû kol ʾănšê hămmilḥamā
10a	kottû ʾittêkæm lăḫᵃrabôt ûmăzmᵉrotêkæm lirmaḥîm
10b	hăḫăllaš jᵉʾomăr gibbôr ʾanî
11a	ʿûšû waboʾû kăl-hăggôjim missabîb wᵉniqbaṣû šammā
11b	hănᵉḫăt jhwh gibbôrặka
12a	jeʿôrû wᵉjăʿᵃlû hăggôjim ʾæl-ʿemæq jᵉhôšapaṭ
12b	kî šam ʾešeb lišpoṭ ʾæt-kăl-hăggôjim missabîb
13a	šilḫû măggal kî bašăl qaṣîr
13b	boʾû rᵉdû kî-malᵉʾā găt
13c	hešîqû hăjᵉqabîm kî răbbā raʿatam
14a	hᵃmônîm hᵃmônîm bᵉʿemæq hæḥarûṣ
14b	kî qarôb jôm jhwh bᵉʿemæq hæḥarûṣ
15	šæmæš wᵉjareaḥ qadarû wᵉkôkabîm ʾasᵉpû nagᵉham
16a	wjhwh miṣṣijjon jišʾag ûmîrûšalăim jitten qôlô
16b	wᵉraʿᵃšû šamăjim waʾaræṣ
16c	wjhwh măḫᵃsæ lᵉʿămmô ûmaʿôz libnê jiśraʾel
17a	wîdăʿtæm kî ʾᵃnî jhwh ʾæelohêkæm šoken bᵉṣijjôn hăr-qådšî
17b	wᵉhajᵉtā jᵉrûšalăim qodæš wᵉzarîm lo-jăʿăbᵉrû-bah ʿôd

Let us note at the outset that 9a—11b is marked by military terminology: milḥamā (9a, 9b); gibbôrîm (10a); gibbôr (10b); gibbôrặka (11b); ḥᵃrabôt (10a); lirmaḥîm (10a). Another conspicuous characteristic is its imperatives and jussives. We are not explicitly told who speaks them nor to whom they are addressed, but 12ab permits the inference that the imperatives are spoken by Yahweh to the gôjim. Because of the imperatives 9a—11a can all be linked at the same level. hănᵉḫăt (11b), although also an imperative, strikes one as peculiar in that it is addressed to Yahweh rather than the gôjim. Since there are no sound text-critical grounds for emendating the text[21], one has to regard this as a parenthetic interlude in which the prophet fleetingly prays to Yahweh.[22] At the same time a certain *Steigerung* is discernible in the successive imperatives: 9a and 9b outline the call to take up arms and the preparations for war; 10ab describes these preparations in more detail, and 11 is the climax: the nations are being called to their own judgment.

Stichs 12a and b are interlinked, the causal kî stating the reason for the jussives (jeʿôrû, jăʿᵃlû) in 12a.

Stichs 13a, b and c are all interlinked at the same level through the series of imperatives (šilḥû -13a; boʾû, rᵉdû -13b; hešîqû -13c), each followed by a causal kî. Another cohesive factor is the harvesting terminology. In 13a and b kî relates to the image used, but in 13c this image is suspended so that the third kî clarifies the first two and explains the real purpose of the imperatives.

14a connects with 14b due to the causal kî at 14b and the striking bᵉʿemæq hæḥarûṣ in both stichs. In 14a the abrupt yet extremely effective hᵃmônîm hᵃmônîm manages to describe the scope and violence of the warfare and the concomitant judgment. This is achieved by repeating the word hamôn, and moreover using its plural.

In the next stichs the close syntactic link between 16a and b is at once apparent: wᵉraʿᵃšû in 16b states the consequence of Yahweh's action in 16a. The synonym parallelism in 16a highlights Yahweh's action. In 16c Yahweh is again the subject, his name is given emphatic prominence and another synonym parallelism occurs. Thus 16c manifestly links up with the preceding lines. The emphatic positioning of Yahweh's name in 16a and c indicates that he plays the key role in these events.[23]

In 17a the person changes dramatically: Israel and Yahweh are no longer referred to in the third person — Yahweh is addressing his people directly. At the same time it emerges that 17b (wᵉhajᵉtā ...) is stating the consequences of šoken bᵉṣijjôn. The repetition of the lexeme qdš in 17b reinforces the connection between 17a and b.

The question is which stich(s) should be linked with 16a–c first — 15 or 17ab? Or should 15 not perhaps first be linked with the preceding 14ab? For three reasons it would seem more logical first to connect *15* with the combination 16abc:

---

[21] Cf. detailed discussion above.
[22] Deden, op. cit., 111.
[23] Verhoef, op. cit., 67.

(a) there is no marked syntactic or semantic link between 15 and the preceding lines;

(b) the person switches dramatically at 17a; and

(c) 16a is linked with the preceding stich by the *waw* copulative.

Thereupon 17ab is overarchingly linked with the preceding lines because it indicates the purpose of Yahweh's action (15–16c): his people should acknowledge him as their God.

Although the *metre* does little to clarify the structure, the staccato rhythm (cf. especially 9a, 13ab) helps to suggest the "hectic arrangements for a military campaign".[24]

Next we must note the *interrelationship* of the various sections (9a–11a, 12a–12b, 13a–c, 14a–b and 15–17b).

12a–b fulfils an important function. It contains some striking repetitions of lexemes from the previous section (cf. haʿîrû – 9a and jeʿôru –12a; jăʿᵃlû – 9b and weʿjăʿᵃlû – 12a; kål-hăggôjim missabîb – 11a and ʾæt-kål-hăggôj missabîb – 12b). These repetitions probably serve to recapitulate the preceding imperatives and define them more closely; also to clarify that the mysterious šammā of 11a is in fact ʾæl-ʿemæq jᵉhôšpaṭ.[25] Thus it emerges that the imperatives in 9a–11b were in effect a summons to judgment (12b).

Stichs 13abc continue the imperatives of 9a–11b. The third person pronominal suffix in 13c (raʿatam) indicates that this stich is once again referring to the gôjim. Hence the third kî in this pericope section (kî raʿatam) is the substantiation for all the imperatives: they concern the wickedness of the gôjim.

One could therefore argue that 12ab serves as a hinge or *nexus* between 9a–11b and 13abc.

Stichs 14ab play a crucial part in the structure of the pericope. The twice repeated beʿemæq hæḥarûṣ clearly refers back to 12a (ʿemæq jᵉhôšapaṭ). ḥarûṣ, as Wolff[26] points out, indicates "das unwiderruflich festgesetzte Vernichtungsurteil". In 14ab it becomes clear that the "vale of judgment" (12a) is in effect a "vale of destruction". Stichs 14ab should be seen as the substantiation for the preceding imperatives,[27] in that it shows that all

---

24 Allen, op. cit., 115; Thomson, IB 6, 756.

25 H.-M. Lutz, op. cit., 58.

26 BKAT XIV/2, 97; cf. also I Reg 20 40; Isa 10 22ff.; Hi 14 5.

27 R. Bach, Aufforderungen zur Flucht und zum Kampf im alttestamentlichen Prophetenspruch, WMANT 9, 1962, 76ff.; H. Irsigler, Gottesgericht und Jahwetag, 328; Lutz, op. cit., 61.

the imperatives and summonses relate to the impending Yom Yahweh. The gôjim are being summoned for the Yom is at hand. Thus in a sense Lutz is right in regarding 4 14 as the key to the entire section,[28] but it is a moot point whether one can call it the climax of the whole chapter.[29]

If one looks at the further development of the pericope one finds that 15—16c describes the Yom. Hence the impending Yom Yahweh of 14ab is not described until 15—16c. Stichs 14ab should therefore rather be seen as the *nexus* between the preceding and succeeding stichs — they also connect with the latter in that the impending Yom (14ab) is described more fully in 15—16c. In view of all this, plus the fact that 17ab has been identified as the goal and object of the whole description of the Yom, we must conclude that 17ab — rather than 14 — is the climax of this pericope section and ultimately of the pericope as a whole.

If one surveys the overall structure of the pericope 4 1—17 one finds that 4 9—17 is the detailed description and amplification of the substance of the first pericope section (cf. especially 2a—3b). This is evident particularly from the repetition of lexemes and phrases (cf. ʾæl-ʿemæq jᵉhôšapaṭ — 2b with 12a and 14ab; wᵉqibbaṣtî ʾæt-kål-hǎggôjim — 2a, with 11a and 12b).

The pericope as a whole also *links* up with the *preceding pericopes*. The introductory formula (4 1) with its accompanying kî not merely refers to the preceding section, but also announces something new: the aforementioned salvation of Israel is reiterated, and is moreover the basis for the judgment to be proclaimed over the nations. This pericope repeats words and phrases from earlier ones, the most striking being 4 14b (kî qarôb jôm jhwh) which flagrantly reflects the conventional Yom Yahweh terminology of 1 15b and 2 1b. Whereas in the first two chapters these terms related to Yahweh's punitive action which included his own people, in this pericope the Yom evidently no longer augurs ill for Israel, but is used in the context of the judgment of the gôjim.

In 4 15 the conventional terminology from 2 10b is repeated. In 2 10b it refers to the cosmic changes accompanying the Yom. Again in contrast to 2 10b, these events bode no harm for Israel.

4 16 repeats the terminology of 2 11a (jitten qôlô), where it depicts Yahweh as the commander of the army. In this pericope it serves to represent him as the source of security for his people during the Yom Yahweh.

The hešîqû hǎjᵉqabîm in 4 13c strongly resembles wᵉhešîqû hǎjᵉqabîm in 2 24. There it describes Yahweh's bounteous blessing to his people,

---

[28] Lutz, op. cit., 61.
[29] Thus Wolff, BKAT XIV/2, 97: Rudolph, KAT XIII/2; Irsigler, op. cit., 61.

whereas in the present pericope it means the exact reverse, namely Yahweh's wrathful action against the gôjim.

All these recurrent phrases serve to stress just one thing: that doom and judgment for Israel has changed to blessing.

One other recurrent phrase remains — 4 17a: wîdă'tæm . . . 'ælohekæm, clearly referring back to 2 27ab, widă'tæm kî bᵉqæræb jiśra'el 'ani wă'ᵃnî jhwh 'ælohêkæm.

Both instances concern the fact that Yahweh's redemptive acts must culminate in the people confessing him as their God.

As for *Gattung*, this pericope could generally be described as an *address by Yahweh*.[30] Throughout he is the speaker, as witness the first person singular verbs and pronominal suffixes. Yahweh's address is interrupted in a few instances only, namely at 11b, 14b and 16a and b. The first instance we have called a parenthetic prayer, the others could probably be explained as conventional forms that are perfectly admissible in an address by Yahweh.

But within this overall *Gattung* one could identify certain other more specific forms. H.-M. Lutz[31] showed that this pericope reflects marked elements of the so called juridical *Gattung*,[32] such as the frequent use of the stem špṭ (2b; 12a, b), all suggesting a lawsuit. Stichs 2a and b may be said to *announce the lawsuit*, and 2c, 3a and b to *list the accused*. Verses 4 4—8 may be identified as a *lively legal argument:*[33] the charge is introduced by the question mah-'ăttæm lî (4b),[34] and through the twofold question in 4c it proceeds to the threat, the "Gegenaktion"[35] being the topic in 7a—8b. Lutz[36] points out that 4 9—12 (especially 12b, 'ešeb lišpoṭ)[37] contains the *verdict* and 4 13ff. the *execution* of this judgment.

Clearly, then, the pericope contains distinct elements of *legal procedure*, although this is not depicted in chronological events. Elements from profane legal procedure are used for the sake of prophetic proclamation, here specifically concerning Jahweh's judgment of the gôjim.

---

[30] Cf. Allen, op. cit., 108:; Wolff, BKAT XIV/2, 88.

[31] Op. cit., 118ff.

[32] For a detailed discussion of this *Gattung* in the Old Testament, cf. H. J. Boecker, Redeformen des Rechtslebens im Alten Testament, ²1970.

[33] Cf. Wolff, BKAT XIV/2, 92.

[34] Cf. e.g. Jdc 8 1; Jer 2 5; Mi 6 3.

[35] Wolff, ibid.

[36] Op. cit., 121, footnote 3.

[37] Cf. also Jdc 4 5; I Sam 22 6; Ex 18 13; Prov 20 8; Ps 122 5.

This juridical *Gattung* provides a framework[38] for another identifiable *Gattung*, for 4 9—13 could be termed an *Aufforderung zum Kampf.*[39] Usually this *Gattung* is marked by the following:[40] (i) calling the warriors to arms; (ii) the preparation of their weapons; and (iii) the military action itself. In 4 9 ff. elements (i) and (ii) are very much in evidence. The passage moreover contains a series of imperatives — another feature of the *Aufforderung zum Kampf*. The original Sitz im Leben of the terminology used here (especially in 9a) was probably the Holy War, but it is doubtful whether the subject matter of this text is a Holy War in the true sense. As mentioned earlier, the *Aufforderung zum Kampf* should be seen within the framework of a juridical *Gattung,* so that the *Aufforderung* is actually a summons to judgment. Hence the object of the imperatives in 4 9 ff. is not Yahweh's gibbôrîm but the nations.[41] Thus the *Gattung* of an *Aufforderung zum Kampf* is here used with heavy irony,[42] strongly stressing Yahweh's judgment of the nations.

From the context it is impossible to discern to whom 4 13 abc is addressed. Is it Israel's actual army, or Yahweh's "heavenly army",[43] or maybe a synergism[44] of the two — possibly even a "figurative"[45] call to an already victorious Israel? Without dismissing the question as trivial ("unerheblich")[46] one must concede that the text does not tell us exactly who is being addressed. What is clear, and vitally significant, is that the speaker is Yahweh and that his actions are focal. C. A. Keller[47] aptly puts it: "Cette grandiose scène du jugement est réalisée par un seul acteur, YHWH. Tous les autres personnages — les foules des nations, les serviteurs de YHWH — ne sont que des comparses". The terminology derived from the Holy War

---

[38] Cf. Lutz, op. cit., 121.

[39] R. Bach, Aufforderungen zur Flucht und zum Kampf im alttestamentlichen Prophetenspruch (WMANT 9), 1962, 51 ff. Cf. also Jer 46 3 ff., 9; 49 14, 28, 31; 50 14 ff., 16, 21, 26 ff., 29.

[40] Cf. Bach, op. cit., especially 62 ff.

[41] Irsigler, op. cit., 328.

[42] Cf. J. Bourke, Le Jour de Jahvé dans Joel, Revue Biblique 66 (1959), 208; Wolff, BKAT XIV/2, 96; Allen, op. cit., 115; H.-P. Müller, Ursprünge und Strukturen altestamentlicher Eschatologie (BZAW 109), 1969, 75.

[43] Cf. P. D. Miller, The divine council and the prophetic call to war, VT 18 (1968), 100—107; Ahlström, SVT XXI, 1971, 70 ff.; Sellin, op. cit., 176; G. Fohrer, Die Propheten des Alten Testaments (Band 6), 1976, 37.

[44] Cf. Irsigler, op. cit., 333, footnote 288.

[45] H.-P. Müller, BZAW 109, 75.

[46] Thus Lutz, op. cit., 58.

[47] Op. cit., 151.

helps to emphasize both the utter destruction of the foe and the fact that Yahweh is actually fighting in person.

The *Aufforderung zum Kampf* comes to an end at 13c, and proceeds via 14ab to what could generally be termed a promise of salvation (16a–17b). The *Gattung* too indicates that we are here concerned with the salvation of Yahweh's people on the one hand and the judgment of the gô-jim on the other.

The pericope contains *traditions* and other conventional material. Stich 2c uses terminology (năḥᵃlatî) reminiscent of the *tradition of the conquest,* although in the present context it is no longer a matter of the physical land Canaan as Yahweh's property, but Israel as his heritage, his own people. The charge against the gôjim is that they violated Yahweh's rights of ownership by scattering his people among the nations.

The *Yom Yahweh tradition* emerges again in 14b. As appears from our analysis, the Yom is here shown as a day of destruction for the nations. By contrast with 1 15 and 2 1ab and 11c, here this tradition does not warn against Yahweh's imminent judgment of his own people, but of the nations. Yahweh's people need not fear the Yom, to them it will be a day of salvation. Thus the Yom Yahweh tradition is used quite differently from the way it features in earlier chapters, clearly indicating that for Israel imminent judgment has changed to salvation.

The *Zion tradition* may also be observed here. Zion is the place from which Yahweh avenges his wrath (16a), wjhwh miṣṣijjon jišᵉag ûmîrûšalăim jitten qôlô. This would appear to be a conventional formula, for it also oc-curs in Am 1 2 (cf. also Isa 25 30). It is remarkable that both in Amos and in Isaiah the expression refers to Yahweh's coming as judge. The author of Joel clearly used traditional material to underscore a weighty matter.

The Zion tradition is also used in close association with the Yom Yah-weh tradition, for stich 16b describes the cosmic upheavals attending that day.

The *Zion tradition* is not used in a negative way only, however. Jerusa-lem is the inviolable sanctuary (17b), never again to be entered by the gô-jim.[48] Jerusalem and Zion are not qadôš in themselves, but only inasmuch as they are the dwelling place and throne of Yahweh[49] (17a). Thus Yahweh

---

[48] Gentiles profaning Yahweh's sanctuary is a conventional Old Testament theme. Cf. e. g. Ps 74 4ff.; 79 1ff. For a detailed discussion of the meaning and incidence of zar in the Old Testament, cf. L. A. Snijders, The meaning of זר in the Old Testament, OTS X, 1954.

[49] A. Kuschke, Die Lagervorstellung der priesterlichen Erzählung, ZAW 63 (1951), 86 refers to the cultic use of škn in the Jerusalem tradition as *terminus technicus* for Yahweh's im-manence in the temple. Cf. also Isa 8 18.

is his people's haven and refuge, their source of security and safety (17). To convey this idea the author once again resorts to conventional cultic terminology closely associated with the Jerusalem theology.[50]

Thus the Zion tradition serves partly to promise salvation to Israel, and partly to pronounce judgment on the gôjim.

The pericope contains other stereotyped material as well. The expression bājjamîm hahemmah ûbaʿet hāhîʾ (4 1) occurs in much the same form in Jer 33 15; 50 4 and 20.[51] Significantly Jer 33 15 uses this formula with reference to a promise of salvation and the security of Jerusalem. In Jer 50 4 the proclamation of the fall of Babylon and a promise of salvation to Judah go hand in hand. The same antithesis may be found in this pericope as well, namely Israel's redemption and judgment on the gôjim.

Verse 4 1 contains another conventional formula, namely ʾašûb ʾæt-šᵉbût.[52] Exegetes are fairly generally agreed that this expression should be interpreted eschatologically, as referring to more than just the return from captivity. As far back as 1895 E. Preuschen wrote:[53] "Freilich hat die Phrase hier bereits einen weiteren Sinn; es ist nicht an die Abwendung des Exils gedacht, sondern an das Ende aller Not, das mit dem Tage Jahves, dem Traum der Zukunft, anbricht." E. L. Dietrich[54] comments: "Das Gericht Jahwes über die גוים gehört in den eschatologischen Vorstellungskreis. . . . In solchem Zusammenhang spielt die Wendung des Exils eine nur nebensächliche Rolle im Vergleich zu den anderen Hoffnungen." G. Fohrer[55] says much the same: "Der Ausdruck begegnet fast ausschließlich in der eschatologischen Theologie und scheint ihr geradezu als stehender Ausdruck für die eschatologische Wiederherstellung zu dienen." In support of this viewpoint Fohrer cites, in addition to Joel 4, the following texts: Dtn 30 3; Jer 29 14; 30 3 and 18; 31 23; 32 14; 33 7, 11, 26; 48 47; 49 6 and 39; Ez 39 25; Am 9 14; Zeph 2 7; 3 20; Ps 14 7 (= 53 7); 85 2; 126 4.

---

[50] Cf. e.g. Ps 14 6; 27 1; 28 8; 37 39; 46 2; 61 4; 62 8ff.; 71 7.

[51] Cf. also Wolff, BKAT XIV/2, 91.

[52] Cf. Holladay, op. cit., 110—114.

[53] Die Bedeutung von שׁוּב שְׁבוּת im Alten Testaments. Eine alte Controverse, ZAW 15 (1895), 65.

[54] שׁוּב שׁבות, Die endzeitliche Wiederherstellung bei den Propheten (BZAW 40), 1925, 24; Cf. also W. Beyerlin, "Wir sind wie Traümende". Studien zum 126. Psalm (Stuttgarter Bibelstudien 89), 1977, 41 who states: "Die Terminus šûb šᵉbût . . . meint nicht die Rückführung deportierter Gefangener".

[55] Die Struktur der alttestamentlichen Eschatologie (in Studien zur alttestamentlichen Prophetie 1949—1965, BZAW 99), 1967, 46—47.

These arguments can probably be upheld. It is certainly true that ʾašûb ʾæt-šᵉbût should be seen as an eschatological formula and a total "Schicksalswende".[56] At the same time it must be realized that the Old Testament promises are not just "pie in the sky". Stichs 2c ("and my heritage Israel ... they have scattered ... among the nations") and 3a ("and have cast lots for my people") — stating the reasons for the lawsuit and, as we have shown, having close syntactic links with the preceding stichs — would appear to refer to the exile. In these verses the author is probably thinking back to the catastrophic events of 733, 721, 597 and 587 B. C.[57] Although theʾašûb ʾæt-šᵉbût transcends the exile and is more than just a promised return from captivity, this turning point nonetheless refers primarily to the crisis caused by the exile. Naturally this eschatological promise would have been highly significant in postexilic times as well.

We must therefore agree with E. Baumann's[58] contention that 4 1ff. refers to the diaspora and the fragmentation of the land. The ʾašûb ʾæt-šᵉbût puts an end to this, but refers not just to the exile, "sondern an das Ende aller Not ...".[59] Note Baumann's observation that wherever this formula occurs, also in Joel 4 1, Yahweh is always "der Autor des Geschehen".[60] Hence the accent is on Yahweh as the one who wrought the change.

It is widely agreed that ʿemæq jᵉhôšapaṭ (2b) is not an ordinary physical valley.[61] The name should rather be interpreted symbolically, as indicated by the striking play on words. ʿemæq jᵉhôšapaṭ is the valley of decision, hence a theological symbol rather than a topographical one.[62] One should seriously consider the idea of A. S. Kapelrud,[63] namely that one could speak of a valley tradition although it might be more correct to call it a *conventional prophetic motif* rather than a tradition. There are no convincing grounds for Kapelrud's contention that the valley tradition belongs to the "sphere of mythology". In Joel this conventional motif is used in keeping with and by way of reinforcement for the judgment of the gôjim.

---

[56] Thus Weiser, op. cit., 123.

[57] Cf. Wolff, BKAT XIV/2, 92.

[58] שוב שבות. Eine exegetische Untersuchung, ZAW 47 (1929), 32.

[59] Ibid., 33.

[60] Ibid., 26.

[61] Cf. e.g. Deden, op. cit., 109; Wolff, BKAT XIV/2, 92; Keller, op. cit., 147; Rudolph, KAT XIII/2, 79; Bič, op. cit., 86; H.-P. Müller, Theologia Viatorum 10 (1965/66), 243; J. Theis, Die Zwölf Kleinen Propheten I, 1937, 101. For a discussion of the problems attached to the "Valley of Jehoshaphat", cf. H. Gressmann, Der Messias, 1929, 115—116.

[62] Allen, op. cit., 109.

[63] Cf. op. cit., 144—147. Kapelrud cites the following corroborative texts: Jer 7 30—34; 19 6; Isa 22; Ez 39; Sach 14.

The expression jaddû gôral (3a) is also part of the "Fremdvölker-worte".[64] This too is a *stereotyped expression*. In Ob 11 it denotes Edom's attack on Jerusalem in 587. In Nah 3 10 it forms part of the judgment on Niniveh. Here in Joel it helps to substantiate the legal action against the nations. Basically the nations are guilty of violating Yahweh's proprietary rights by casting lots over his people, dividing them as prisoners of war and treating them as their property.

Stich 10a ("Beat your ploughshares into swords, and your pruning hooks into spears") neatly inverts the *conventional motif* found in Isa 2 4 and Mi 4 3 ("and they shall beat their swords into ploughshares, and their spears into pruning hooks"). As mentioned earlier, this parody of Isa 2 4 and Mi 4 3 renders the *Aufforderung zum Kampf* highly ironical. The author is using traditional material but in his own individual manner. The inversion of the stereotyped motif serves to indicate that what awaits the nations is not salvation, but doom and destruction. The irony of the presentation underscores the severity of the judgment.

From this survey it is evident that the pericope has garnered a rich hoard of traditional material, something which could help to date the book of Joel.

Once again the *redaction history* of the pericope relates to that of the book as a whole.[65] A few "internal" redactional problems also call for attention, starting with verse 4 1. Bewer[66] regards this verse as a "connecting link" inserted by a later redactor to join the preceding pericope with what follows. Jepsen[67] maintains that it is an addition by the "apocalyptic" redactor, while R. E. Wolfe[68] attributes not just 4 1 but 4 1–3 to the "Day of Yahweh Editor". Our analysis has shown 4 1 to be a conventional introductory formula which – not only in Joel but also in Jer 33 15 and Jer 50 4 and 20 – is integral to the promise of salvation to God's people and the judgment of the gôjim. For this reason, and in the absence of adequate proof to the contrary, it would be inadvisable to see 4 1 simply as a connection link added by a later hand.

The redaction history of 4 4–8 have however been subject to most speculation. Let us consider some of the more important arguments. Be-

---

[64] Wolff, BKAT XIV/2, 92.
[65] Cf. discussion of this point in the section on the redaction history of 3 1–5. Cf. also W. S. Prinsloo, NGTT XXIV (1983), 255 ff.
[66] Op. cit., 127.
[67] ZAW 56 (1938), 86.
[68] ZAW 53 (1935), 103.

wer[69] writes: "These verses are . . . a later insertion by a writer who probably interpreted vv. 2.3 as referring to the Persians under Artaxerxes Ochus,
c. 352 B. C. He added them here because the behaviour of the Phoenicians
and Philistines at that time called for special condemnation. They were the
traders and merchants to whom the Persian soldiers had sold their captives
and their booty". Bewer fails to explain, however, precisely why he regards
4—8 as an insertion. Deden[70] maintains that this passage reminds one of an
interpolation protesting against possible preferential treatment of Phoenicia
and Philistia. Weiser[71] sees 4 4—8 as an interpolation between 4 1—3 and 4
9 ff. He describes it as a piece of prose which "wahrscheinlich erst nachträg-
lich der Joelprophetie eingefügt worden ist". This scholar too fails to specify his grounds for regarding 4 4—8 as an interpolation and merely claims
that it is "wahrscheinlich". Interestingly, R. E. Wolfe[72] who sees 4 4—8 as a
redactional insertion, claims that the "anti-neighbor Editor" inserted 4
4—11 and 13 as well. G. Fohrer[73] regards 4 4—8 as a "jüngerer Einschub"
and O. Kaiser[74] likewise describes it as a later addition which he therefore
leaves out of account in his dating of the book. R. Smend[75] calls 4 4—8 an
"unzweifelhaften Prosazusatz". H. W. Wolff was the first to substantiate
in detail his claim that 4 4—8 is a later insertion. His principal arguments
are:[76]

(i)   It interrupts the continuity between 4 1—3 and 9 ff.
(ii)   Its literary style is all its own and only the *Stichwort* mkr links it to
        the preceding section.
(iii)   Whereas the context refers to the gôjim generally, here Tyre, Sidon
        and Philistia are addressed directly.
(iv)   In 4 2 ff. Yahweh speaks of "my people", "my heritage", "my
        land", but here he refers to b^enê j^ehûdā.
(v)   The idea of retribution is foreign to the book of Joel.
(vi)   The rhetorical questions and word repetitions are alien to the rest of
        Joel.
(vii)   The sentences are longer and contain more subordinate clauses than
        those in the earlier and subsequent passages.

---

[69] Op. cit., 130.
[70] Op. cit., 109.
[71] Op. cit., 123.
[72] ZAW 53 (1935), 96—97.
[73] Das Alte Testament 2/3, 1970, 78.
[74] Einleitung in das Alte Testament, ³1975, 258.
[75] R. Smend, Die Entstehung des Alten Testaments I, 1978, 172.
[76] Wolff, BKAT XIV/2, 89—90. Cf. also Deissler (NEB), 83.

H.-P. Müller[77] is very much in agreement with Wolff, observing: "Die
den Zusammenhang störenden prosaischen Sätze 4:4—8 werden allgemein
als Nachtrag angesehen". P. Höffken[78] also concurs with Wolff and points
out that 4 4—8 belongs to a different intellectual climate from that of
preceding and subsequent parts. By this he means mainly that it is less apocalyptic than the rest of chapter 4, and should therefore rather be considered historical.[79] W. Rudolph[80] has a different view: he too sees 4 4—8 as a
"störender Einschub" mainly because it does not fit in with the apocalyptic
tone of the rest of the chapter and the rhythm of the prose is different from
that of chapter 4 as a whole. But unlike most exegetes Rudolph does not see
this as the latest addition to the book, and hence does not consider it inau-
thentic. He writes:[81] "Ich sehe deshalb keine Bedenken, auch 4:4—8 der
letzten vorexilischen Zeit zuzuweisen, so daß nichts dagegen spricht, Joel
für den Verfasser zu halten." In his view 4 4—8 might originally have appeared after 4 21 and could have been moved to its present position later in
order to effect a "Stichwortanordnung" (mkr) with the preceding passage.

Clearly one's ideas about the redaction history of Joel 4 4—8 will greatly affect one's *dating of the book as a whole*. Hence a brief orientation is
necessary: when one scrutinizes the different exegetes' views on this problem it is sometimes hard to tell what comes first, the chicken or the egg!
This applies to both the exponents of a pre-exilic dating and those who date
Joel after the exile: is 4 4—8 dated pre-exilically simply because the particular exegete has dated the rest of the book before the exile and was therefore
more or less obliged to do the same in the case of 4 4—8? Or is this passage
dated pre-exilically on manifest textual grounds? Conversely, is 4 4—8 dated after the exile and hăjjᵉwanîm equated with the Greeks because the exegete had preconceived notions about a pre-exilic dating? Or does the text
make it clear that hăjjᵉwanîm refers to the Greeks?

Many exegetes see the mention of hăjjᵉwanîm as definite proof of the
postexilic origin of Joel.[82] Rudolph[83] however found that this expression

---

[77] Theologia Viatorum 10 (1965/66), 244.
[78] Untersuchungen zu den Begründungselementen der Völkerorakel des Alten Testaments,
1977, 82—83.
[79] Ibid., 437, footnote 232.
[80] KAT XIII/2, 80—81.
[81] Rudolph, KAT XIII/2, 82.
[82] Cf. e.g. J. Morgenstern, The testimony of Joel 4:2b—8, 19—20, HUCA XXVII (1956),
150—153; Bo Reicke, Joel und seine Zeit (Wort-Gebot-Glaube, Walter Eichrodt zum 80.
Geburtstag), Abhandlungen zur Theologie des Alten und Neuen Testament, vol. 59, 1970,

occurs in eighth-century Assyrian inscriptions as well; according to him excavations have shown that they had relatively frequent contact with Palestine in the seventh and sixth centuries. Hence he does not regard 4 6 as conclusive evidence for a postexilic dating of Joel, and — partly on the basis of 4 4—8 — favours a late pre-exilic dating.[84] A. S. Kapelrud made the same point some time before Rudolph did, pointing out[85] that the hăjjᵉwanîm "was thus well known throughout the entire Near East already at the end of the 8th century and certainly during the 7th". Kapelrud[86] also claims — which brings us back to redaction history — that 4 4—8 affords no grounds for regarding it as a later insertion. Possibly it is best to let Kapelrud speak for himself:[87] "It has also been possible to point out that the historical events, possibly alluded to in the section, by no means need to be dated to the 4th or 3rd century or still later. They are in part not appropriate to that period and can otherwise be readily explained as pertaining to about the year 600 and after. It is thus not on historical grounds that the section should be dated to more recent times, nor is this necessary for linguistic or religio-historic reasons."

All this once more underscores the relativity and subjectivity of attempts at dating a book. In my opinion Rudolph and Kapelrud are quite right in maintaining that it is risky to date 4 4—8 after the exile purely on the strength of the reference to hăjjᵉwanîm. On the other hand they overplay their hand when they use hăjjᵉwanîm as ground for an exclusively pre-exilic dating, ruling out a postexilic date. We find, therefore, that hăjjᵉwanîm is used as evidence for both a pre-exilic and a postexilic dating, implying that one should be wary of relying too heavily on 4 4—8 for an exact dating.

There are other reasons, however, for indicating that a postexilic dating would be safe. As Smend points out:[88] "4:1—3 setzt die seit dem Exil bestehende Situation überdeutlich voraus." If one has to be even more precise, Joel would seem to point to a date after the reconstruction of the tem-

---

140; Wolff, BKAT XIV/2, 93; Duhm, ZAW 31 (1911), 188 goes so far as to claim that 4 4ff. refers to Maccabean times.

[83] KAT XIII/2, 81—82; cf. also I. H. Eybers, "Dating Joel's Prophecies", ThEv 5—7 (1972—1974), 215: "There is enough evidence that the Greeks were definitely known in the Near East in pre-exilic times ...".

[84] Rudolph, KAT XIII/2, 82.

[85] Op. cit., 154—155.

[86] Op. cit., 159. Cf. also Ahlström, SVT 21 (1971).

[87] Ibid.

[88] Die Entstehung des Alten Testaments I, 1978, 172.

ple (cf. 1 9, 14, 16; 2 14; 4 18). It would therefore be reasonably safe to date
Joel after 515 when the temple was rebuilt. The frequency of conventional
material and "quotations" from other prophetic books is also a general
pointer to a postexilic origin. But to use 2 7 and 9 as evidence that the book
must have originated after the construction of the city walls in 445 is reading too much into the text. One cannot be certain that 2 7 and 9 are referring
to the city walls,[89] and besides, it was pointed out above that 2 1—11 presents a dramatic, hyperbolical account. It would therefore be inadvisable to
deduce concrete historical facts from a passage of this nature.

A postexilic dating for the book of Joel is assured. One could even
fairly confidently posit a date of origin after 515 B. C., but since the text
itself offers no concrete evidence it is safer — albeit perhaps unsatisfactory
— to content oneself with this somewhat vague indication of a date some
time after 515.

This broad orientation permits us to sum up the redaction history of 4
4—8. Most of the scholarly arguments for regarding 4 4—8 as a later insertion (see discussion above) are convincing. But the tendency to denigrate
the importance of this passage on these grounds and to treat it as peripheral
derives from the (mistaken!) romantic notion that the earliest text is necessarily the true, the best and most authoritative text. Our premise here is that
4 4—8 forms part of the text as we have it today and should therefore be
taken seriously. The insertion of this passage fulfilled a certain function and
adds a new dimension to the text. Besides, 4 4—8 is not as remote from the
context as some scholars would have it be.[90] Our analysis has shown that
both structurally and substantively it fits very well into the context (cf. argument above). Hence it is no mere arbitrary insertion, but a piece of com-
petent, deliberate editing, apparently aimed at concretizing and specifying
the vague, general assertions of the preceding pericope section (1—3a). Proclaiming Yahweh's wrathful treatment of the gôjim would have been a fitting message for the catastrophic period after the exile.

We must add some further comments on the redaction history. True to
his method, Wolfe[91] regards 4 12 and 4 14—17 as additions by his "Day of
Yahweh Editor". There is no real reason to take his proposals seriously — it
is simply impossible to trace the minutiae of the redactional process as
Wolfe tries to do. The same may be said of Jepsen[92] who claims that 14b,

---

[89] Cf. Eybers, ThEv 5—7 (1972—74), 217.
[90] Cf. e.g. Höffken, op. cit., 83.
[91] ZAW 53 (1935), 103.
[92] ZAW 56 (1938), 87.

the beginning of 16a, 16b and 17b are products of the so-called apocalyptic redactor. Robinson calls 4 15—17 a short apocalyptic poem concocted from diverse ingredients,[93] and his view is supported by H.-P. Müller.[94] Kapelrud, however, pointed out that Robinson's diagnosis contained a contradiction in terms, in that he speaks of "zusammengeflickt" on the one hand, but at the same time of an independent poem "das als eine Originalschöpfung gelten könnte, wenn wir die Quellen nicht kennen, aus denen sein Material genommen ist".[95] The author undeniably made liberal use of conventional material, but it is impossible to identify all his "sources" exactly. Neither does it do justice to the passage to refer to it as a concoction or a mosaic. As our analysis has shown, 4 15—17 constitute a meaningful whole with a specific function in the compositional structure of the pericope (cf. discussion above).

Our exegesis now permits us to arrive at some conclusions about the *theology* of this passage, which relates very closely to the preceding one. The salvation depicted in the latter is developed further, and Yahweh emerges as the author of the total change in the crisis afflicting his people.

This promise of salvation to God's people provides the springboard for a judgment on the gôjim. Once again Yahweh's action is paramount. Three successive verbs (2a, 2b) climactically indicate that judgment is the real purpose of Yahweh's activity. He is both prosecutor and judge, but in his judgment he is neither arbitrary nor fickle. The blame is placed squarely on the gôjim, whose guilt is affirmed by a succession of no fewer than six verbs. Basically the gôjim are guilty of violating Yahweh's proprietary rights: he is Lord of his land and his people, and the gôjim have trespassed on both.

In 4 4—8 the case is expressed far more concretely. The nations who ignore Yahweh's proprietorship and thereby dishonour him must know that their deeds will boomerang. The rhetorical questions (4bc) once again affirm the guilt of the nations beyond all doubt. Their offence against Yahweh's rights of ownership is reiterated (5, 6a). Yahweh continues to feature as the principal character. He is the one who will visit the nations' misdeeds upon them: because they sold Yahweh's people into slavery (6) Yahweh will sell them as slaves (8a), they caused Yahweh's people to be far from their own land (6b) and Yahweh will see that the same thing happens to them (8b). Hence the roles will be reversed, with Yahweh bringing the

[93] Robinson, op. cit., 68, clearly borrowed the term "zusammengeflickt" from Duhm. Cf. Duhm, ZAW 31 (1911), 188.
[94] Cf. Theologia Viatorum 10 (1965/66), 247.
[95] Robinson, op. cit., 68.

change. Just as he changes his people's fortunes for the better, he will repay
the gôjim for their sins by judging them.

This train of thought is contained in the next pericope section. Yahweh's omnipotence is expressed by his call to the nations. The string of
imperatives in 4 9 ff. — formally a call to arms using terminology derived
from the Holy War — is in effect a summons to judgment. This gives the
passage a heavily ironical tone which underscores the severity of the judgment on the nations. The irony is even more flagrant in 4 10a, a parody on
Isa 2 4 and Mi 4 3 which neatly inverts the conventional imagery. It is clearly a summons not merely to judgment but to destruction (14a, 14b). The
harvesting images with the accompanying imperatives stress the finality of
the judgment. As in the previous pericope the sins of the gôjim (13c) are
cited as the grounds for Yahweh's judgment.

Throughout these events Yahweh is the principal character. Everything relates to his imminent coming, the Yom Yahweh.

This Yom is a day of destruction for the gôjim, but by contrast with
the earlier parts of Joel (1 5; 2 1 ff.) it no longer bodes evil for Yahweh's
people. This day, marked by cosmic upheaval, will bring doom and destruction for the gôjim, but salvation for Israel. Thus there is a clear progression in the use of the Yom Yahweh tradition in Joel, vividly indicating
that doom and disaster have changed to salvation. The Zion tradition is also
accommodated within this framework: *on the one hand* it is the seat from
which Yahweh avenges his wrath on the nations, *on the other* it is a place of
security and salvation for his people by virtue of being his abode. The syntactic prominence of Yahweh's name (16a, 16c) yet again accentuates his
acts: he determines what happens.

Stichs 17ab, a repetition of 2 27b, is the climax of the pericope. *Here it
is shown that the ultimate goal of Yahweh's deeds in the world is that his
people should acknowledge him as the God of the covenant.* As in 2 27b, the
confession of Yahweh's people is not unsubstantiated but is based on his
deeds. The two issues that form the backbone of this pericope — Yahweh's
judgment of the gôjim and his blessing of his people — must have been of
tremendous significance in the crisis situation of the postexilic cultus.

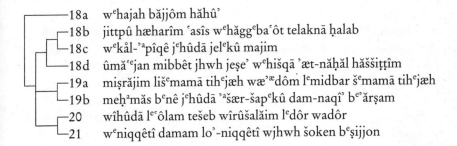

18a   wᵉhajah băjjôm hăhû'

18b   jittpû hæharîm ʿasîs wᵉhăggᵉbaʿôt telaknā ḥalab

18c   wᵉkål-'ᵃpîqê jᵉhûdā jelᵉkû majim

18d   ûmăʿᵉjan mibbêt jhwh jeṣe' wᵉhišqā 'æt-năḥăl hăššiṭṭîm

19a   miṣrăjim lišᵉmamā tihᵉjæh wæ'ᵆdôm lᵉmidbar šᵉmamā tihᵉjæh

19b   meḥᵃmăs bᵉnê jᵉhûdā 'ᵃšær-šapᵉkû dam-naqî' bᵉᵉărṣam

20   wîhûdā lᵉᵉôlam tešeb wîrûšalăim lᵉdôr wadôr

21   wᵉniqqêtî damam lo'-niqqêtî wjhwh šoken bᵉṣijjon

The stereotyped formula wᵉhajah băjjom hăhû' not only introduces a new pericope but also connects it to the preceding one.

This pericope contains one *text-critical* problem worth noting. If wᵉ-niqqêtî damam lo'-niqqêti (21a) is rendered as it stands it makes no sense. Consequently scholars have tried to emendate the text or find alternative translations to solve the problem. The following are among the more meaningful attempts: One answer is to read the first phrase as a question and the second as a negative response.[1] A second solution, which actually does not quite fit the context, is to follow the Vulgate in rendering the verb with "cleanse" or "reconcile".[2] The fact that the Vulgate translates it with the same verbs is a fair indication that the Hebrew must also have had two resembling verbs — hence an affirmation of the Massoretic text. W. Rudolph,[3] following Driver, renders the stem nqh, by analogy with the Akkadian *niqū*, with "poured out": "Und ich werde ihr eigenes Blut ausgießen, das ich (bisher) nich ausgegossen habe …". The blood is said to refer to Egypt and Moab and Yahweh's punishment of them. There are two reasons why this suggestion is unacceptable. Firstly, as it appears in the Massoretic

---

[1] Cf. Allen, op. cit., 117: "And shall I leave their bloodshed unpunished? I will not …". Cf. W. Nowack, Die kleinen Propheten, (HAT III/4), 1903, 117 for reservations about this solution.

[2] Cf. e. g. A. Weiser, ATD 24, 122: "Und sühnen werd' ich ihr Blut, das noch nicht ich gesühnt".

[3] SVT 16 (1967), 250; KAT XIII/2, 76.

text today, damam refers to the preceding and to Jerusalem — and surely Yahweh's punishment is not aimed at them. Secondly there is no direct proof of a connection between the verb niqqêti and the Akkadian *niqū*.

Another solution, apparently following the LXX and Syriac versions, is to change niqqêti into niqqamtî, hence "I will avenge their blood".[4] However, both Allen[5] and Rudolph[6] point out that the LXX use of ekdikein for *nqh* in Sach 5 3 makes this proposal — changing niqqêti to niqqamtî — unlikely. This textual change is normally accompanied by one of two alternatives. The change obviously relates to the second word, lo'-niqqêtî, which is then, analogously to LXX changed to w^{e}lo'-'^{a}naqqæh[7] ("I shall not leave unpunished"); a second possibility is to change lo'-niqqêti into niqǎmti as well.[8]

The likeliest solution is to read lo' as la', that is as an emphatic or affirmative particle.[9] There are two advantages to this reading. Firstly, it does not require any textual emendation, but merely a change in vocalization. Besides 4 21 is clearly a repetition of and play on dam-naqî' in 19b. The above solution would accord well with such a pun. The function of an emphatic repetition of niqqêti would be to stress that the blood of Judah and Jerusalem was shed innocently.

Since there are no other text-critical problems of any magnitude we turn to the *structure* of the pericope. Stichs 18bcd are linked chainwise: Stichs 18b and c are linked by the corresponding imperfect plural verbs (jitt^{e}pû, telaknā — 18b; jel^{e}kû — 18c). Note the stem hlk which appears in both stichs. The *waw* copulative links 18d with the preceding lines. As far as content goes, the criterion is the paradisial image starting in 18b which is continued and terminated in 18d. In 18d a consequence clause featuring a perfect consecutive depicts the eventual outcome of the preceding paradisial situation: the valley of Shittim will also be watered.

At 19a the subject changes and the paradisial image terminates. Syntactically 19b connects closely with 19a. The min in 19b substantiates the situation in 19a. The third person plural verb (šap^{e}kû) also refers to Egypt and Edom in 19a. There is a dramatic contrast between 19ab and the preceding stichs.

---

[5] Op. cit., 117, footnote 47.   [4] Cf. BHS ad loc.; BHK³ ad loc.

[6] KAT XIII/2, 78, footnote 21d; SVT 16 (1967), 250.

[7] Cf. BHS ad loc.; BHK³ ad loc.; Thompson, IB, 760.

[8] Deden, op. cit., 114; G. W. Wade, The books of the Prophets, Micah, Obadiah, Joel and Jonah, 1925, 119; Bewer, op. cit., 144; Robinson, op. cit., 68.

[9] Keller, op. cit., 153. Cf. also Kapelrud, op. cit., 175; Ahlström, SVT 21 (1971), 95—96 also settles for this reading but accepts "pour out" as the meaning of nqh.

The antithetic *waw* (wihûdā) links 20 with 19 in vivid contrast. The first half stich of 21 strikes one as peculiar owing to the startling switch to a first person singular verb, so much so that one could even wonder whether it is not perhaps a later redactional addition (see discussion below). Nonetheless 21 as it stands has firm links with the preceding stichs. Firstly the *waw* copulative connects it with 20 and secondly, the third person plural suffix (damam) takes up again the Judah and Jerusalem of 20. There are thus clear links between the two stichs.

The three pericope sections 18bcd, 19ab, and 20/21 are all connected at the same level. The *waw* at 21 (wjhwh šoken . . .) should probably be considered affirmative — "Yes, Yahweh indeed dwells in Zion". The participle (šoken) accentuates the perpetual character of Yahweh's occupancy.

A few other points should be raised concerning the interrelationship of the three sections. Robinson[10] shows that two themes may be traced in 4 18—21, namely *salvation for Judah* and *retribution against its enemies*. In his view these motifs are arranged chiastically:[11]

A 18   Salvation for Judah
B 19   Vengeance on the enemy
A 20   Salvation for Judah
BA 21   Vengeance on the enemy/Salvation for Judah

But do both these themes in fact occur in 21 as Robinson maintains? It seems rather as if this stich refers only to Judah (that is, A) which has to be declared innocent. At most one could argue that element B features indirectly. But even if one concedes Robinson's point as regards the pattern of the motifs, this structure (A, B, A, BA) cannot be called a chiasmus in the full sense of the word. In addition Robinson omits to state the function of the alleged chiasmus, but uses it merely to counter Bewer's and Sellin's view of the redaction history (see discussion below).

Hence the structure needs to be analysed more subtly than Robinson has done. We have pointed out that 19ab is antithetical to 18bcd. In addition 20/21 is the antithesis of 19ab. If one examines the three stich sections overall and takes content as one criterion, it would seem more like a case of *symmetry:*[12]

---

[10] Robinson, op. cit., 69.
[11] Robinson, op. cit., 69. He is supported by Ahlström, SVT 21 (1971), 95—96.
[12] C. A. Keller, op. cit., 152 is therefore correct in saying: "Le poème est composé selon le principe fondamental de la symétrie: Juda — Egypte/Edom — Juda/Jérusalem". One must be careful, however, not to overlook the fact that these are not the only names used. After

Salvation for Judah (18bcd) A
Doom for Egypt and Edom (19ab) B
Salvation for Judah (20/21) A

This structure, although accentuating the doom on Egypt and Edom, compensates with the twofold salvation for Judah.

In the nature of things 18a connects overarchingly with 18b—21.

By contrast with the rest of Joel this pericope with very few exceptions has a regular 3 + 3 *metre*.[13]

There are several conspicuously repeated *words and phrases*, starting with the stem hlk in 18b and c. In conjunction with the other verbs in 18bcd it expresses the dynamic nature of the salvation events. šᵉmamā is markedly repeated twice in 19a, heavily emphasizing the desolation to be visited on Egypt and Edom. The proper noun Judah occurs no fewer than thrice. We have already mentioned that the first halfline of 21 repeats the end of 19b.

Lexemes from other pericopes also recur here, the most striking being šoken bᵉṣijjon (21) which establishes a direct link with the preceding pericope (cf. 4 17a). This shows the tremendous significance of Yahweh's dwelling in Zion.

The lᵉdôr wadôr in 20 also features regularly in Joel (cf. 1 3b; 2 2d). In the two earlier instances it relates to the extraordinary nature of the catastrophe, however, whereas here its context is one of continuing salvation.

Other lexeme recurrences also effect a contrast: ʿasîs appears in 1 5a in the context of a call to lamentation, whereas in 4 18b it forms part of a promise and describes superabundance.

Similarly ʾᵃpiqîm in 1 20b occurs in a context of arid drought; in 4 18c it is part of a description of bounty and plenty of water.

The author/redactor uses these repetitions to emphasize the progression in the course of the book. Doom has changed to salvation, drought and calamity to blessing and prosperity. Hence the beginning of the book contrasts sharply with the end.

The *Gattung* of the pericope may be described as an *eschatological promise of salvation*, the salvation being intensified by the accompanying prophecy of doom for Egypt and Edom.

Egypt/Edom (19b) Judah is mentioned again (19b) before the combination Judah/Jerusalem (20) recurs.

[13] Cf. Allen, op. cit., 116—117; Robinson, op. cit., 69; Bewer, op. cit., 141; Keller, op. cit., 153.

The text offers no direct clues to the *Sitz in Leben*. Kapelrud's view,[14] namely that the pericope has its *Sitz* in the cultus, more specifically the so-called enthronement feast, derives from subjective exaggeration of the role of the cultus and is therefore unacceptable.

To infer a direct dating from the mention of Egypt and Edom (19a) is equally risky. Does the m^{e}ḥ^{a}mās b^{e}nê j^{e}ḥûdā refer to specific atrocities perpetrated on Judah by Egypt and Edom? In the case of Egypt, does it for instance refer to events at the time of the exodus or those in 609 B. C.? And in the case of Edom, does it refer specifically to Edom's role in the events of 587?[15] The text offers no clues. But even if one could establish precisely which historical events are intended, it would not help us to discover the historical *Sitz in Leben* of the *author* of the text. As the references to Egypt and Edom stand in the text today it is best to interpret them simply as indicating that these were Judah's number one enemies. Within the framework of the aforementioned *Gattung* Egypt and Edom serve as a dramatic contrast to Judah, thus underscoring the copious blessings bestowed on the latter.

Like the rest of the book, this pericope draws on *traditions* and other stereotyped material. The *Zion tradition* once again features prominently (cf. 21), expressed in the same terminology (šoken b^{e}ṣijjon) as in the previous pericope. The repetition stresses the significance of this statement. Within the structure of the pericope the wjhwh šoken b^{e}ṣijjon also plays an important part. Being the final half line of the pericope, and preceded as it is by an affirmative *waw* it is heavily emphatic. The promises of salvation manifestly depend on the Zion tradition. The copious blessings are directly associated with Yahweh's active presence in Zion. He is the author of all these blessings. Everything proceeds from him, and his presence in Zion is a determining factor. C. A. Keller[16] observes: "C'est la présence de YHWH qui assurera la fertilité du pays de Juda et la prospérité de ses habitants."

Other conventional material includes the introductory formula w^{e}haj-ah băjjôm hăhû'[17]. H.-M. Lutz[18] points out that in the Old Testament this expression is not a technical formula for the Yom Yahweh, and this probably applies to this incidence in Joel as well. Elsewhere in Joel where the

---

[14] Cf. op. cit., 166 ff.
[15] Cf. op. cit., Ob 10 ff.; Ps 137 7.
[16] Op. cit., ad loc.
[17] Cf. e. g. also Isa 7 18, 21, 23; 10 20, 27; 11 10, 11; 17 4; 22 30; 23 15; 24 21; 27 12, 13; Jer 4 9; 30 8; Ez 38 10, 18; 39 11; Hos 1 5; 2 18, 23; Am 8 9; Mi 5 9; Zeph 1 10; Sach 12 3, 9; 13 2, 4; 14 6, 8, 13.
[18] WMANT 27, 130.

Yom Yahweh is referred to, it is mentioned so explicitly as to leave no room for doubt. In this case wᵉhajah bǎjjom hǎhûʾ formally introduces a new pericope but substantively it is a temporal expression specifically referring to the eschatological age.

The motif of *paradisial eschatology* also appears here — the end-time is described in terms reminiscent of paradise. The hyperbolical image of mountains oozing with sweet wine and hills flowing with it is a stereotyped image of blessing and bounty,[19] as is the expression (18c) that the dry river beds of Judah will be flooded with water. In 18c there is another element of paradisial eschatology, namely the stream of life flowing from the temple. This is another conventional image frequently found in the Old Testament.[20] Although Joel is using conventional material, he does so in his own distinctive manner. Here the accent is on the fact that the temple, the abode of Yahweh, is the fount of all blessings. Hence in actual fact Yahweh is the giver of fertility and blessings.

Despite various attempts to establish the location of the nǎḥǎl hǎssiṭṭîm (18d)[21] the text contains no definite geographical information. Sellin[22] is probably quite right when he says: "Die Sache liegt vielmehr genau so wie bei dem Tale Josaphat, es handelt sich ja hier um eine Geographie der Endzeit."

The function of these conventional paradisial eschatological motifs is, however, quite clear: they are meant to accentuate the radical and total change awaiting Yahweh's people. Weiser[23] aptly sums it up: "Diese Bilder

---

[19] Cf. Am 9 13 "'Behold the days are coming', says the Lord, 'when ... the mountains shall drip sweet wine and all the hills shall flow with it'". Cf. also Gen 49 11.

[20] Cf. Ez 47 1—12; Sach 14 18; Ps 46 5; 65 10; Isa 33 21; Gen 2 10ff.

[21] Following Num 25 1 and 33 49 Merx, op. cit., 75 associates it with Shittim in Moab. Bewer, op. cit., 142 associates it with Wādi-es-Sanṭ about 30 km west of Jerusalem. This location would mean that, contrary to what one finds in Ezekiel, the temple stream flows in a westerly direction.
As may be expected Kapelrud, op. cit., 170—171 (followed by Bič, op. cit., 102) offers a cultic explanation. He does not attempt to physically locate the "valley of acacia trees", but interprets it against a cultic background: the acacia was "closely associated with the sanctuaries and the sacred objects ... Therefore it must not be lacking in Israel's beatific time to come ... And for these acacia-trees Yahweh will provide".
A popular solution is to see it as the dry Wādi-en-Nar, the extension of the Kidron valley which runs down to the Dead Sea. Cf. Thompson, IB 6, 760—761; Keller, op. cit., 154; Wolff, BKAT XIV/2, 101; Allen, op. cit., 124).

[22] Op. cit., 177. Sellin's proposal (177—178) that hǎššiṭṭîm should be changed to hǎššedîm (i.e. vale of demons) is quite unfounded.

[23] Weiser, ATD 24/1, 126.

sind entsprungen aus dem Glauben, daß dem allmächtigen Gott alle Wege
und Wunder des gesamten Schöpfungsbereichs zur Verfügung stehen; sie
sind gleichzeitig die endgültige Offenbarung seiner Wundermacht in Ver-
bindung mit seinem gnädigen Heilswillen und binden so Anfang und Ende
der Welt zusammen in dem eindrucksvollen Hymnus auf die Macht der
Gnade Gottes . . .".

The paradisial eschatological motifs in 4 18 contrast vividly with 1 10
and 1 20 where the context is one of drought and aridity. This illustrates the
development occurring in the course of the book.

The *redaction history* of 4 18–21 is by no means clear. For one thing,
there is a possibility that the entire pericope is a later addition.[24] If one accepts this explanation, the question remains: does this passage derive from
the author of the book Joel himself, or from someone who deliberately co-
pied his language?[25] The text itself does not provide an answer to this question, but the fact is that 4 18–21 links up very well both with the preceding
pericope and with the rest of the book, for instance the lexemes repeated
from the preceding pericope and elsewhere in the book. We must agree
with Childs[26] (as opposed to Wolff) that the unity of the book does not
necessarily indicate a single author. It might also have been a result of deliberate redaction. For our purpose, however, it is sufficient to note that the
pericope occupies an important place in the compositional structure of Joel:
here the book reaches a climax, and this pericope is moreover in deliberate
contrast to the beginning of Joel.

The *redaction history* of individual stichs or stich sections has also giv-
en rise to comment. R. E. Wolfe[27] believes that 4 18 and 19 and the first part
of 21 are the work of the "Eschatologists", and 4 20 and the latter part of 21
are attributable to the "Psalm Editor".[28] These views are based on an un-
proven, subjective assumption – the existence of a number of editors – and
is therefore unacceptable. Jepsen[29] attributes 4 18–20 to the "apocalyptic"
redactor.

The original sequence of the stichs has also been disputed, in particular
the original position of the first half line of 21 (wᵉniqqêtî damam loʾ-niqqê-
ti). The view that this halfline originally followed 19b has considerable sup-

---

[24] Thus Wolff, BKAT XIV/2; R. Rendtorff, Das Alte Testament, Eine Einführung, 1983, 231
    appears to agree with this view.

[25] Cf. Wolff, BKAT XIV/2, 90.

[26] Introduction, 387 ff.

[27] ZAW 53 (1935), 105.

[28] Ibid, 112.

[29] ZAW 56 (1938), 87.

port,[30] but most of its exponents fail to take proper account of the function of the text as it stands today. In response to this view — notable as expressed by Sellin and Bewer — Robinson[31] pointed out the deliberate structuring and coherence of the pericope, also affirmed by our analysis. But structure and coherence — even in this narrow context — does not necessarily imply a single author, so that one will probably have to agree with Wolff[32] that the halfline of 21 was a later addition designed to supply a final theological clarification. The terminology was deliberately adapted to conform with 19b. The function of the addition was probably to show that Yahweh wants to redress the injustice of the shedding of his people's innocent blood.

Let us now consider the *theology* of this final pericope of Joel. Our analysis has revealed two cardinal issues, namely *salvation for Judah* and *doom for the enemies*. Hence in this sense the theme of the preceding pericope is resumed and elaborated further.

Symmetrical structure strongly accentuates the doom on Egypt and Edom, but this is offset by the two promises of salvation to Judah, depicted in paradisial-eschatological images. Blessings and abundance will be the share of the Lord's people. The barren land will flow with water. Significantly the temple, the abode of Yahweh, is the fount of all these blessings, so that in effect Yahweh is the origin of it all, the giver of good gifts. The pericope contrasts with the beginning of the book. Aridity, drought and food shortages have made way for fertility and plenty. The temple, once deprived of offerings, has become the fount of blessings. Calamity has changed to salvation and prosperity.

There is also a progression in the form these blessings take. In the first part of the symmetrical structure (18b—d) we are apparently dealing with abundance and fertility in *nature*. In the third part (20—21) we appear to be concerned with *political deliverance:* Judah will "sit", will dwell in safety and security. The Zion tradition is invoked once again to show that it is Yahweh's presence in Zion that vouchsaves Judah's safety. Where Yahweh

---

[30] Cf. Sellin, op. cit., 178; Bewer, op. cit., 143: "It is evident that a sentence like this has no real place after vv. 9ff. It stood originally directly after v. 19b". Duhm, ZAW 31 (1911), 188 comments thus: "Der Satz v. 21a, ... gehört mindestens nicht an seinem jetzigen Ort, sondern eher, wenn der Ergänzer ihn geschrieben hat, hinter v. 19, ...". Rudolph, KAT XIII/2, 78 transposes the whole of 21 to after 19.

[31] Op. cit., 69. Even though Robinson's structural analysis of the pericope may not be altogether correct (cf. the discussion above), he nonetheless pointed out its logical coherence as it stands today. Robinson is supported by Kapelrud, op. cit., 175.

[32] Cf. Wolff's arguments in BKAT XIV/2, 102.

dwells his people will find their home.[33] Yahweh is the source, guarantee and author of the blessings. He is in the midst of his people. There is an indissoluble link between his presence among them and the concrete blessings that will befall them.

Thus the book of Joel ends on a triumphal note[34]. Yahweh dwells in Zion, the judgment is past, the catastrophe has been averted and changed to salvation. This eschatological theology must have offered great comfort in the difficult times after the exile.

In direct contrast to this is the fate of Egypt and Edom. Because they shed Judah's blood their territories will be turned to wilderness. The roles are reversed. Egypt, normally a fertile place owing to the presence of the Nile, will become a desert. Judah, an arid land, will flow with water.

We must reiterate that Yahweh is the one who effects both the doom and the salvation, so that in this respect the book of Joel is intensely theocentric.

[33] Wolff, BKAT XIV/2, 102.
[34] Cf. Robinson, op. cit., 69.

XI. The theology of the book of Joel: Summary

To form a picture of the theology of the entire book one needs to survey its overall structure and the interrelationship of the various pericopes.

Since Wolff contributed greatly to the case of the unity of the book some critical comments on his view of it is called for.

One has to concede Wolff's point that Joel constitutes a unity, but does he see that unity correctly? He speaks of a "nahezu vollendete Symmetrie der beiden Teile",[1] these "Teile" being 1 2–2 17 and 2 18–4 21. Wolff's conception of the structure of Joel is as follows:[2]

A   1 4–20   (Lament over the want of sustenance)
B   2 1–11   (Announcement of an eschatological catastrophe in Jerusalem)
C   2 12–17   (Call to return to Yahweh "als dem vorläufig Notwendigen".)

A   2 21–17   (End of want of sustenance)
C   3 1–5   (Spirit poured out and salvation on Zion "als das eschatologisch Notwendige …")
B   4 1–3; 9–17 (End of eschatological crisis)

This representation of the structure of the book calls for comment. It is at once evident that the structure is not symmetrical in the fullest sense. It would have been symmetrical if elements A, B and C had occurred in the same sequence in both parts of the book. It is not clear whether Wolff was referring to this somewhat assymetrical trait when he spoke of "nahezu vollendete Symmetrie".

The idea of a symmetrical structure obviously stands or falls by the division of the book into two parts, namely 1 2–2 17 and 2 18–4 21. We have pointed out that 2 18 is not quite the "turning point" it is commonly

---

[1] BKAT XIV/2, 6.
[2] Ibid.

accepted to be (cf. discussion above, 63 ff.). Although 2 18 marks the start of a new pericope, neither as regards form nor as regards content does it represent a definite break with the preceding part. Nor is the promise of blessing and gracious conduct of Yahweh a new element in 2 18 ff., for both were anticipated in the preceding pericope (2 12—17).

One further comment on Wolff's portrayal of the structure of Joel: he conspiciously omits 2 18—20; 4 4—8; and 4 18—21 from his schema, evidently confining himself to passages which he considers to derive from Joel's own hand. But since we are concerning ourselves with the final form of the book we must ask how these verses would have fitted into the symmetrical structure. Thus 2 19 might also have been classifiable as "End of want of sustenance". And could 3 1—5 — which Wolff classifies as "Spirit poured out, salvation on Zion" — not also have been included under "End of eschatological crisis"?

Thus Wolff's alleged symmetry appears to be a relative one and the unity of the book will have to be demonstrated in some other way.

It would be better to depict the structure of the book so that the various pericopes interrelate in a step-by-step progression, each representing a *Steigerung* on its precursor. Virtually all the pericopes refer — through word and phrase repetitions — to a previous pericope or pericopes. As a result each pericope is not merely linked with the ones immediately preceding and following it, but is integrated into a whole which all the more clearly reveals the ascending pattern, in itself identifiable as a contrast. Hence the final pericope should be seen as the climax of the book.

Thus the structure of the book may be depicted as follows: 1 1 is obviously the heading of the entire book. The following diagram should be read in conjunction with the substantiation:

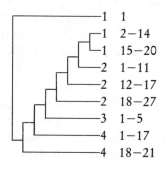

```
———————————1  1
          ┌1  2—14
          ├┐
          └1  15—20
         └2  1—11
        ┌2  12—17
       ┌┤
      ┌┤2  18—27
     ┌┤3  1—5
    ┌┤4  1—17
    └└4  18—21
```

In view of the above comments and our exegesis of the individual pericopes, the *theology of the book of Joel* could be summarized thus.

Joel is a *theocentric book,* as witness the heading (1 1) which refers to everything below it as authoritative words of Yahweh. In the rest of the book as well, as it proceeds from lamentation to a promise of salvation, from calamity to a hopeful future, Yahweh is the "main character".

The first pericope (1 2−14) describes the extensive nature of the catastrophe which strikes the entire community. The locust plague is not interpreted purely as a natural disaster, but as a call to repentance. Neither are farming and cultic life separate compartments. The agricultural crisis affects relations with Yahweh as well. But in this crisis Yahweh is not a *Deus otiosus:* the land and the people are his. He is with them in their suffering. The call for a national lament has as its real purpose a cry of distress to Yahweh. Hence the locust plague and attendant catastrophe point the way back to Yahweh.

The second pericope (1 15−20) concerns an even more dire calamity, namely the impending Yom Yahweh. This is no peaceful, tranquil day but forms part of Yahweh's punitive action. The accent is on Yahweh's mighty initiative. He brought about the crisis. By describing the portents of the Yom Yahweh analogously to the plague of locusts the author makes it clear that this plague and everything associated with it are also portents of the Yom Yahweh. These portents afflict the entire community and the day is inescapable. Man and beast alike suffer under the catastrophe, resulting in a common cry of distress to Yahweh. The call for lamentation (1 5−14) is intensified to an actual cry of distress to Yahweh, so that this second pericope too may be classified as theocentric.

In the next pericope (2 1−11) the Yom features even more prominently. It is depicted as a gloomy, ominous day. Although the wrath of Yahweh starts among his own people, the Yom has international and cosmic repercussions. The main point is that Yahweh personally commands the devastating army. He is actively intervening. The theophanic terminology indicates that we are dealing with the coming of Yahweh himself. The alarm therefore serves to warn Yahweh's people. Here the Zion tradition fulfils a warning function.

The alarm proceeds to turn into a call for repentance (2 12−17) issued by Yahweh himself. His word heralds the turning point, he takes the initiative in the dialogue culminating in repentance. It is an urgent appeal for wholehearted repentance to be expressed palpably. The repentance must be directed to Yahweh, who is not a strange God but 'ᵃlohêhæm. The appeal is based on Yahweh's love, grace and mercy. The possibility of repentance derives not from the people, but from the grace of Yahweh. The hymnic description helps to accentuate the greatness and might of the Lord. Hence after the cry of alarm in 2 1–11 we have a call to repentance in 2 12–17. It appears that the Yom Yahweh and Yahweh's imminent coming are aimed not at the destruction of his people but at their conversion to him. Yet there is no causal connection between the people's repentance and Yahweh's response: he is not to be pressurized by their remorse, his freedom cannot be curbed. Hence there is a polarity between Yahweh's threatening anger and his gracious intervention. This pericope raises the hope that Yahweh will extend his blessing and create new possibilities of life for his people. The tradition of the promise of the land is used as grounds for imploring Yahweh's intervention on behalf of his people lest they be put to shame before the nations.

Pericope 2 18–27 again shows a *Steigerung* on the preceding pericope. The call for repentance becomes an *Erhörungswort*, the dawning hope is realized: the "perhaps" (2 14) is fulfilled. It is made perfectly clear that the change was wrought by Yahweh. His action is emphasized. It is he who causes the hope to be fulfilled. His action consists in restoring to his people the basic sustenance they need to live. This terminates the crisis that prevailed. Yahweh has changed doom to salvation, drought and famine to prosperity. Relations with his people are normalized. His action also means that his people will never again be put to shame by the nations.

Yahweh is the one who brings about the utter destruction of the enemy who commits the sin of hubris. The significant point is that Yahweh has personally ordered this enemy to move against his own people. Hence he will turn even on his own "punitive agent" should this latter exalt himself against the Lord.

Yahweh's promise of salvation leads to an urgent call to his people to rejoice. Yahweh's action results in joy: his gracious intervention is cause for the hymnic summons. The entire cosmos is called to praise the Lord.

The earth, the beasts, Yahweh's own people all join in a single chorale of praise. The emphasis is, however, on the $b^e n\hat{e}$ ṣijjôn. The relationship between Yahweh and his people is restored: he is their God.

This pericope too focuses sharply on Yahweh's acts, which consist in promises to compensate his people for the calamity wrought by the locusts. Yahweh sent the disaster to his people, but he also puts an end to it. Once again it is stressed that through his intervention his people will have plenty to eat. But this removal of the crisis is not an end in itself: he who eats in abundance must know to praise abundantly. Yahweh must be given thanks. He has done the impossible, the miraculous by changing calamity into blessings and prosperity, nor will his people ever be put to shame again. The pericope culminates in the credal formula (2 27a) which is naturally firmly founded on Yahweh's mighty deeds. His redemptive deeds move his people to confess him. The substance of the creed describes Yahweh as one who is with his people. He alone is God: there is none beside him.

3 1–5 are closely connected with the preceding pericope but also announce a new era of salvation for Israel. The accent is once again squarely on Yahweh's acts. He takes the initiative and the outpouring of his rûăḥ determines events. Just as he had infused fresh vitality by pouring out bounteous rains, so he instils vitality with the outpouring of his rûăḥ, which is given to his whole people irrespective of age, sex or social status. The entire nation consists of fully authorized media of revelation. The Yom Yahweh no longer bodes peril and doom (cf. 2 1–11) for Yahweh's people but becomes a day of salvation. The môpᵉtîm, portents of the Yom, are signs of his extraordinary acts of salvation for his people. It is, so to speak, a new exodus. The promised era of salvation is given a new dimension when the Zion tradition is invoked to point out that in Yahweh there is security and safety. But the promise of salvation is not unqualified. Yahweh wants no mere lip service but confession in word and deed.

The next pericope again connects with the preceding one. Salvation is amplified, Yahweh is described further as the one who will completely transform the crisis of his people.

The promise of salvation provides a springboard for the judgment of the gôjim, on whom the blame is squarely placed. Their fault is basically that they have violated Yahweh's proprietary rights (over his land and his people). These acts of the gôjim will boomerang: Whatever they did to Yahweh's people and property will be done to them. Hence the roles are reversed and once again Yahweh is the one to effect the change. Just as he changed the fortunes of his people for the better, so he will repay the wickedness of the gôjim. This judgment over the gôjim is given an edge by the ironic call to a Holy War which is really a summons to destruction. In all these events Yahweh is the principal character. His actions are associated with the Yom, that day of judgment for the gôjim, but of salvation for Yahweh's people. Stich 4 17a makes it clear that the ultimate aim of his works is that his people should acknowledge him as the God of the covenant. Once again the creed is based firmly on Yahweh's actions.

Two things are focal in this final pericope: the two promises of salvation to Judah and the doom on Judah's foes. Yahweh effects both salvation and doom, but for his people there is only prosperity and salvation. The temple is the fount of all these blessings. This final pericope contrasts dramatically with the beginning of the book: calamity has changed to deliverance. The pericope reveals an indissoluble link between Yahweh's presence among his people and the concrete blessings that will befall them. Hence the book ends on a triumphal note: Yahweh dwells in Zion. The judgment is past, the catastrophe averted.

It seems as if a crisis situation (a plague of locusts) occurring after the exile was interpreted theologically and then used in these grim times to kindle fresh hope for the future.

Bibliography

Aalders, G. C., Oud Testamentische Kanoniek, 1952.

Ahlström, G. W., Hāmmōreh liṣdāqāh in Joel II 23, SVT 17 (1969), 25–36.

–, Joel and the temple cult of Jerusalem, SVT 21 (1971).

Albright, W. F., Review of R. H. Pfeiffer, Introduction to the Old Testament, JBL 61 (1942) 120f.

Allen, L. C., The books of Joel, Obadiah, Jonah and Micah, NICOT, 1976.

Bach, R., Aufforderungen zur Flucht und zum Kampf im alttestamentlichen Prophetenspruch, 1962.

Baumann, A., יָלַל, ThWAT Band III, 1981, 6–7.

Baumann, E., שׁוּב שְׁבוּת, Eine exegetische Untersuchung, ZAW 47 (1929), 17–44.

Baumgartner, W., Joel 1 und 2, BZAW 34, 1920.

Beek, M. A., Inleiding in de Joodse Apokalyptiek van het Oud- en Nieuw-Testamentisch Tijdvak, Theologia VI, 1950.

Begrich, J., Das priesterliche Heilsorakel, ZAW 52 (1934), 81–92.

Bewer, J. A., The Book of Joel, ICC, 1974.

Beyerlin, W., "Wir sind wie Träumende", Studien zum 126. Psalm, (Stuttgarter Bibelstudien 89), 1977.

Bič, M., Das Buch Joel, 1960.

Birkeland, H., Zum hebräischen Traditionswesen. Die Komposition der prophetischen Bücher des Alten Testaments, 1938.

Boecker, H. J., Redeformen des Rechtslebens im Alten Testament, [2]1970.

Bourke, J., Le Jour de Jahvé dans Joël, RB 66 (1959), 5–31 and 91–212.

Brongers, H. A., Der Eifer des Herrn Zebaoth, VT 13 (1963), 269–284.

Budde, K., "Der von Norden" in Joel 2, 20, OLZ 22 (1919), 1–5.

–, Der Umschwung in Joel 2, OLZ 22 (1919), 104–110.

Černy, L., The day of Yahweh and some relevant problems, 1948.

Chary, Ch., Les Prophètes et le Culte à partir de l'exil, (Bibliothèque de Thèologie III/III), 1955.

Childs, B. S., The enemy from the north and the chaos tradition, JBL 78 (1959), 187–198.

–, Introduction to the Old Testament as Scripture, 1979.

Clements, R. E., Old Testament Theology, A fresh approach, 1978.

Credner, K. A., Der Prophet Joel, 1831.

Dahood, M., The four cardinal points in Psalm 75,7 and Joel 2,20, Biblica 52 (1971), 397.

–, Hebrew-Ugaritic Lexicography IX, Biblica 52 (1971), 342.

Deden, D., De kleine profeten, BOT, 1953.

Deissler, A., Zwölf Propheten, Hosea. Joel. Amos, NEB 4, 1981.

Deist, F. E., Prior to the dawn of apocalyptic, OTWSA 25 (1982)/OTWSA 26 (1983), 13–38.

Dennefeld, L., Les problèmes du livre de Joël, RSR 4 (1924), 555–575.

Dentan, R. C., The literary affinities of Exodus XXXIV 6f., VT 12 (1963), 34–51.

Dietrich, E. L., שׁוּב שְׁבוּת, Die endzeitliche Wiederherstellung bei den Propheten, BZAW 40, 1925.

Duhm, B., Theologie der Propheten, 1875.

—, Anmerkungen zu den Zwölf Propheten, ZAW 31 (1911), 184–188.

—, Israels Propheten, ²1922.

Edwards, G., The Exodus and Apocalyptic, (in A Stubborn Faith, Presented to W. A. Irwin), 1956.

Everson, A. J., The Days of Yahweh, JBL 93 (1974), 329–337.

Eybers, I. H., Dating Joel's Prophecies, ThEv 5–7 (1972–1974), 199–223.

Fensham, F. C., A possible origin of the concept of the Day of the Lord, Biblical Essays 1966 – Proceedings of the Ninth meeting of "Die Ou-Testamentiese Werkgemeenskap in Suid-Afrika", 90–97.

Fohrer, G., Die Struktur der alttestamentlichen Eschatologie, in Studien zur alttestamentlichen Prophetie 1949–1965, BZAW 99, 1967.

—, Das Alte Testament 2/3, 1970.

—, Die Propheten des Alten Testaments, 1976.

Frankfort, T., Le כִּי de Joel I 12, VT 10 (1960), 445–448.

Frey, H., Das Buch der Kirche in der Weltwende, BAT 24, 1948.

Frost, S. B., Old Testament Apocalyptic, 1952.

Gese, H., Geschichtliches Denken im Alten Orient und im Alten Testament, ZThK 55 (1958), 127–145.

—, Kleine Beiträge zum Verständnis des Amosbuches, VT 12 (1962), 417–438.

—, Anfang und Ende der Apokalyptik dargestellt am Sacharjabuch ZThK 10 (1973), 20–49.

Gressmann, H., Der Ursprung der israelitisch jüdischen Eschatologie, 1905.

—, Der Messias, 1929.

Hanson, P. D., The dawn of Apocalyptic, 1975.

Hasel, G. F., Old Testament Theology, Basic issues in the current debate, ³1982.

Hardmeier, C., Texttheorie und biblische Exegese (Beiträge zur evangelischen Theologie, Band 79), 1978.

Höffken, P., Untersuchungen zu den Begründungselementen der Völkerorakel des Alten Testaments, 1977.

Hoffmann, Y., The Day of the Lord as a concept and a term in the prophetic literature, ZAW 93 (1981), 37–50.

Holladay, W. L., The root šûbh in the Old Testament, 1958.

Holzinger, H., Sprachcharakter und Abfassungszeit des Buches Joel, ZAW 9 (1889), 89–131.

Horst, F., Zwei Begriffe für Eigentum, in Verbannung und Heimkehr (W. Rudolph zum 70. Geburtstage), 1961, 135–156.

Humbert, P., Problèmes du livre d'Habacuc, 1944.

Hyatt, J. P., The peril from the north in Jeremiah, JBL 59 (1940), 499–513.

Irsigler, H., Gottesgericht und Jahwetag, Die Komposition Sef. 1, 1–2, 3, untersucht auf der Grundlage der Literarkritik des Zefanjabuches, 1977.

Janzen, W., Morning cry and woe oracle, BZAW 125, 1972.

Jepsen, A., Kleine Beiträge zum Zwölfprophetenbuch, ZAW 15 (1938), 85–96.

Jeremias, J., Theophanie, Die Geschichte einer alttestamentliche Gattung, WMANT 10, ²1977.

Jones, D. R., Isaiah 56–66 and Joel, Torch Bible Commentaries, 1964.

Kaiser, O., Einleitung in das Alte Testament, ³1975.

Kapelrud, A. S., Joel Studies, 1948.

Keller, C. A., Joël, Abdias, Jonas, Commentaire de l'Ancien Testament XI/a, 1965.

Kèrrigan, A., The "sensus plenior" of Joel III, 1–5, in Act., II, 14–36, Sacra Pagina II, – Bibliotheca Ephermeridum Theologicarum Lovaniensum 12/13 (1959), 295–315.

Kritzinger, J. H., Die profesie van Joël, 1935.

Koch, K., Die Propheten I, Assyrische Zeit, 1978.

Kuschke, A., Die Lagervorstellung der priesterlichen Erzählung, ZAW 63 (1951), 74–105.

Kutsch, E., Heuschreckenplage und Tag Jahwes in Joel 1 und 2, TZ 18/2 (1962), 81–94.

Lindblom, J., ThLZ 90 (1965), 424.

Louw, J. P., Semantiek van Nuwe Testamentiese Grieks, 1976.

Lutz, H.-M., Jahwe, Jerusalem und die Völker, WMANT 27, 1968.

Lys, D., "Ruach" le souffle dans l'Ancien Testament, 1962.

Malamat, A., Mari and The Bible: Some patterns of tribal organization and institutions, JAOS 82 (1962), 148ff.

Mallon, E. D., A stylistic analysis of Joel 1:10–12, CBQ 45 (1983), 537–548.

Marti, K., Das Dodekapropheton, 1904.

Meiden, L. H. van der, De vertaling van het woord morêh in Joël 2:23, GTT 51 (1951), 137–139.

Merx, A., Die Prophetie des Joel und ihre Ausleger von den ältesten Zeiten bis zu den Reformatoren, 1879.

Meyer, R., Melchisedek von Jerusalem und Moresedek von Qumran, SVT 15 (1966), 228–239.

Miller, P. D., The divine council and the prophetic call to war, VT 18 (1968), 100–107.

Morgenstern, J., The testimony of Joel 4:2b–8, 19–20, HUCA XXVII (1956), 150–153.

Mowinckel, S., Psalmenstudien, Buch I–II, 1961.

Müller, H.-P., Prophetie und Apokalyptik bei Joel, Theologia Viatorum 10 (1965/66), 231–252.

–, Ursprünge und Strukturen alttestamentlicher Eschatologie, BZAW 109, 1969.

Myers, J. M., Some considerations bearing on the date of Joel, ZAW 74 (1962), 177–195.

Nestle, E., Miscellen I. Joel 1, 17, ZAW 20 (1900), 164–165.

Noth, M., Das Geschichtsverständnis der alttestamentlichen Apokalyptik, Theologische Bücherei 6, ³1966.

Nowack, D. W., Die kleinen Propheten, HAT III/4, ³1922.

Ogden, G. S., Joel 4 and prophetic responses to national laments, JSOT 26 (1983), 97–107.

Osten-Sacken, P. von der, Die Apokalyptik in ihrem Verhältnis zur Prophetie und Weisheit (Theologische Existenz Heute nr. 157), 1969.

Plath, M., Joel 1 15–20, ZAW 47 (1929), 159–160.

Plöger, O., Theokratie und Eschatologie, 1959.

Preuschen, E., Die Bedeutung von שְׁבוּת שׁוּב im Alten Testaments. Eine alte Controverse, ZAW 15 (1895), 1–74.

Prinsloo, W. S., Jahwe die Vrymagtige, 1976.

–, The Theology of the book of Ruth, VT 30 (1980), 330–341.

–, The Theology of Jeremiah 27:1–11, OTWSA 24 (1981), 67–83.

–, Isaiah 14 12–15 – Humiliation, Hubris, Humiliation, ZAW 93 (1981), 432–438.

–, Die boek Joël: verleentheid of geleentheid?, NGTT XXIV (1983), 255–263.

Procksch, O., Die kleinen prophetischen Schriften nach dem Exil, 1916.

Rabinowitz, I., The guides of righteousness, VT 8 (1958), 391–404.

Rad, G. von, The origin of the concept of the Day of Yahweh, JSS IV (1959), 97–108.

–, Theologie des Alten Testaments II, ⁵1968.

Raitt, T. M., The prophetic summons to repentance, ZAW 83 (1971), 30–49.

Reicke, B., Joel und seine Zeit, Wort-Gebot-Glaube, Walter Eichrodt zum 80. Geburtstag, Abhandlungen zur Theologie des Alten und Neuen Testaments 59, 1970.

Rendtorff, R., Das Alte Testament, Eine Einführung, 1983.

Reventlow, H. G., Grundfragen der alttestamentlichen Theologie im Licht der neueren deutschen Forschung, TZ 17 (1961), 81–93.

–, Prophetisches Ich bei Jeremia, 1962.

–, Hauptprobleme der alttestamentlichen Theologie im 20. Jahrhundert, Erträge der Forschung Band 173, 1982.

Richter, W., Exegese als Literaturwissenschaft, Entwurf einer alttestamentlichen Literatur Theorie und Methodologie, 1971.

Robinson, T. H., Die Zwölf Kleinen Propheten, HAT 14, ³1964.

Roth, C., The teacher of righteousness and the Prophecy of Joel, VT 13 (1963), 91–95.

Rothstein, J. W., in Einleitung in die Literatur des Alten Testaments (S. R. Driver), 1896.

Rudolph, W., Ein Beitrag zum hebräischen Lexikon aus dem Joelbuch, SVT 16 (1967), 244–250.

–, Wann wirkte Joel?, BZAW 105 (1967), 193–198.

–, Joel – Amos – Obadja – Jona, KAT XIII/2, 1971.

Saebø, M., יום II–VI, ThWAT Band III/6–7, 1980, 566–586.

Scharbert, J., Formgeschichte und Exegese von Ex 34 6f. und seiner Parallelen, Biblica 38 (1957), 130–150.

Schmidt, J. M., Die jüdische Apokalyptik, 1969.

Schunk, K. D., Strukturlinien in der Entwicklung der Vorstellung vom "Tag Jahwes", VT 14 (1964), 319–330.

–, Die Eschatologie der Propheten des Alten Testaments und ihre Wandlung in exilisch-nachexilischer Zeit, SVT 26, 1974.

Seebaß, H., Biblische Theologie, Beihefte zu EvTh 1 (1982), 28–45.

Sellers, O. R., A possible Old Testament reference to the teacher of righteousness, IEJ 5 (1955), 93–95.

Sellin, E., Das Zwölfprophetenbuch, ³1929.

Smend, R., Die Entstehung des Alten Testaments, 1978.

Snijders, L. A., The meaning of זר in the Old Testament, OTS X, 1954.

Sprengling, M., Joel 1, 17a, JBL 38 (1919), 129–141.

Steck, O. H., Überlegungen zur Eigenart der spätisraelitischen Apokalyptik, Die Botschaft und die Boten – Festschrift für H. W. Wolff, 1981, 301–315.

Stephenson, F. R., The date of the book of Joel, VT 19 (1969), 224–229.

Theis, J., Die Zwölf Kleinen Propheten I, Die Heilige Schrift des Alten Testaments VIII, Band 3/1, 1937.

Thompson, J. A., The Book of Joel, IB 6, 1956.

–, The use of repetition in the prophecy of Joel, On language culture and religion: In honor of E. A. Nida, 1956.

Treves, M., The date of Joel, VT 7 (1957), 224–229.

Verhoef, P. A., Die Dag van die Here, Exegetica 11/3, 1956.

Vernes, M., Le peuple d'Israël et ses espèrances, 1872.

Vosloo, W., Op soek na die oorsprong van die begrip "Die dag van die Here", ThEv (Sept. 1975), 183–198.

Vriezen, Th. C., Prophecy and Eschatology, SVT 1, 1953.

Wade, G. W., The books of the Prophets Micah, Obadiah, Joel and Jonah, 1925.

Weingreen, J., The title moreh ṣedek, JSS VI (1961), 162–174.

Weippert, M., "Heiliger Krieg" in Israel und Assyrien. Kritische Anmerkungen zu Gerhard von Rads Konzept des "Heiligen Krieges im Alten Israel", ZAW 84 (1972), 460–493.

Weiser, A., Das Buch der Zwölf Kleinen Propheten, ATD 24/1, 1956.

Weiss, M., The origin of the "Day of the Lord" – reconsidered, HUCA 37 (1966), 28–60.

Westermann, C., Struktur und Geschichte der Klage im Alten Testament ZAW 66 (1954), 44–80.

Whitley, C. F., ʿbṭ in Joel 2, 7, Biblica 65 (1984), 101–102.

Willi-Plein, I., Das Geheimnis der Apokalyptik, VT 27 (1977), 62–81.

Wolff, H. W., Das Thema 'Umkehr' in der alttestamentlichen Prophetie, ZThK 48 (1951), 129–148.

–, Der Aufruf zur Volksklage, ZAW 76 (1964), 48–56.

–, Die Botschaft des Buches Joel, Theologische Existenz Heute 109, 1963.

–, Dodekapropheton 1, Hosea, BKAT XIV/1, ²1965.

–, Dodekapropheton 2, Joel und Amos, BKAT XIV/2, ²1975.

Wolfe, R. E., The Editing of the book of the Twelve, ZAW 53 (1935), 90–129.

Woude, A. S. van der, Micha, POT, 1976.

Young, E., An Introduction to the Old Testament, 1949.

Zimmerli, W., Erkenntnis Gottes nach dem Buch Eseschiël, 1954.

Index to Scripture References

BEIHEFTE ZUR ZEITSCHRIFT FÜR DIE ALTTESTAMENTLICHE WISSENSCHAFT

LUDWIG SCHMIDT

De Deo

Studien zur Literaturkritik und Theologie des Buches Jona,
des Gesprächs zwischen Abraham und Jahwe in Gen 18, 2ff.
und von Hi 1

Groß-Oktav. VIII, 198 Seiten. 1976. Ganzleinen DM 104,–
ISBN 3 11 006618 1 Band 143)

KONRAD RUPPRECHT

Der Tempel von Jerusalem

Gründung Salomos oder jebusitisches Erbe?

Groß-Oktav. X, 109 Seiten. 1977. Ganzleinen DM 57,–
ISBN 3 11 006619 X (Band 144)

AUGUST STROBEL

Der spätbronzezeitliche Seevölkersturm

Ein Forschungsüberblick mit Folgerungen
zur biblischen Exodusthematik

Groß-Oktav. XII, 291 Seiten. 1976. Ganzleinen DM 116,–
ISBN 3 11 006761 7 (Band 145)

PETER WEIMAR

Untersuchungen zur Redaktionsgeschichte des Pentateuch

Groß-Oktav. X, 183 Seiten. 1977. Ganzleinen DM 86,–
ISBN 3 11 006731 5 (Band 146)

ROLF RENDTORFF

Das überlieferungsgeschichtliche Problem des Pentateuch

Groß-Oktav. VIII, 177 Seiten. 1977. Ganzleinen DM 87,–
ISBN 3 11 006760 9 (Band 147)

Preisänderungen vorbehalten

Walter de Gruyter Berlin · New York

BEIHEFTE ZUR ZEITSCHRIFT FÜR DIE ALTTESTAMENTLICHE
WISSENSCHAFT

CHARLES F. WHITLEY

Koheleth

His Language and Thought

Large-octavo. VIII, 199 pages. 1979. Cloth DM 96,–
ISBN 3 11 007602 0 (Volume 148)

INGRID RIESENER

Der Stamm עבד im Alten Testament

Eine Wortuntersuchung unter Berücksichtigung
neuerer sprachwissenschaftlicher Methoden

Groß-Oktav. VIII, 294 Seiten. 1978. Ganzleinen DM 155,–
ISBN 3 11 007260 2 (Band 149)

Prophecy

Essays presented to Georg Fohrer on his sixty-fifth birthday
6. September 1980.
Edited by J. A. Emerton

Large-octavo. VIII, 202 pages, Frontispiece. 1980. Cloth DM 92,–
ISBN 3 11 007761 2 (Volume 150)

GERALD SHEPPARD

Wisdom as a Hermeneutical Construct

A Study in the Sapientializing of the Old Testament

Large-octavo. XII, 178 pages. 1980. Cloth DM 78,–
ISBN 3 11 007504 0 (Volume 151)

J. A. LOADER

Polar Structures in the Book of Qohelet

Large-octavo. XII, 138 pages. 1979. Cloth DM 69.50
ISBN 3 11 007636 5 (Volume 152)

Preisänderungen vorbehalten

Walter de Gruyter Berlin · New York

BEIHEFTE ZUR ZEITSCHRIFT FÜR DIE ALTTESTAMENTLICHE
WISSENSCHAFT

WALTER BEYERLIN

Werden und Wesen des 107. Psalms

Groß-Oktav. XII, 120 Seiten. 1978. Ganzleinen DM 73,–
ISBN 3 11 007755 8 (Band 153)

HANS CH. SCHMITT

Die nichtpriesterliche Josephsgeschichte

Ein Beitrag zur neuesten Pentateuchkritik

Groß-Oktav. XII, 225 Seiten. 1979. Ganzleinen DM 86,–
ISBN 3 11 007834 1 (Band 154)

GEORG FOHRER

Studien zu alttestamentlichen Texten und Themen

Groß-Oktav. X, 212 Seiten. 1981. Ganzleinen DM 84,–
ISBN 3 11 008499 6 (Band 155)

CHRISTA SCHÄFER-LICHTENBERGER

Stadt und Eidgenossenschaft im Alten Testament

Eine Auseinandersetzung mit Max Webers Studie
„Das antike Judentum"

Groß-Oktav. XII, 485 Seiten. 1983. Ganzleinen DM 108,–
ISBN 3 11 008591 7 (Band 156)

CLAUS PETERSEN

Mythos im Alten Testament

Bestimmung des Mythosbegriffs und Untersuchung
der mythischen Elemente in den Psalmen

Groß-Oktav. XVIII, 280 Seiten. 3 Tabellen. 1982. Ganzleinen DM 88,–
ISBN 3 11 008813 4 (Band 157)

Preisänderungen vorbehalten

Walter de Gruyter   Berlin · New York

BEIHEFTE ZUR ZEITSCHRIFT FÜR DIE ALTTESTAMENTLICHE
WISSENSCHAFT

PHILIP J. NEL

The Structure and Ethos of the Wisdom Admonitions in Proverbs

Large-octavo. XII, 142 pages. 1982. Cloth DM 74,–
ISBN 3 11 008750 2 (Volume 158)

GEORG FOHRER

Studien zum Buche Hiob (1956–1979)

Zweite, erweiterte und bearbeitete Auflage
Groß-Oktav. XII, 146 Seiten. 1983. Ganzleinen DM 72,–
ISBN 3 11 008967 X (Band 159)

OSWALD LORETZ

Habiru-Hebräer

Eine sozio-linguistische Studie über die Herkunft
des Gentiliziums ʿibrî vom Appellativum ḫabirū

Groß-Oktav. XV, 314 Seiten. 1984. Ganzleinen DM 106,–
ISBN 3 11 009730 3 (Band 160)

OTTO KAISER

Der Mensch unter dem Schicksal

Studien zur Geschichte, Theologie
und Gegenwartsbedeutung der Weisheit

Groß-Oktav. X, 292 Seiten. 1985. Ganzleinen DM 98,–
ISBN 3 11 010095 9 (Band 161)

Bibel und Alter Orient

Altorientalische Beiträge zum Alten Testament
von Wolfram von Soden

Herausgegeben von Hans-Peter Müller
Groß-Oktav. XII, 224 Seiten. 1985. Ganzleinen DM 96,–
ISBN 3 11 010091 6 (Band 162)

Preisänderungen vorbehalten

Walter de Gruyter

Berlin · New York